# LEADING AT THE SPEED OF GROWTH

# LEADING AT THE SPEED OF GROWTH

JOURNEY

FROM

ENTREPRENEUR

TO

CEO

KATHERINE CATLIN
& JANA MATTHEWS

FIRST IN A SERIES OF BOOKS ON MANAGING GROWTH
FROM THE
KAUFFMAN CENTER FOR ENTREPRENEURIAL LEADERSHIP

Hungry Minds, Inc.
Cleveland, OH • Indianapolis, IN • New York, NY

# HUNGRY MINDS, INC.

909 Third Avenue
New York, NY 10022

ISBN 0-7645-5366-6

Library of Congress Control Number:  2001089295

*Editor:* Pamela Sourelis
*Production Editor:* M. Faunette Johnston
*Designer:* Michael Rutkowski
*Production by Hungry Minds Indianapolis Production Services*

## SPECIAL SALES

For general information on Hungry Minds' products and services please contact our Customer Care department: within the U.S. at 800-762-2974, outside the U.S. at 317-572-3993 or fax 317-572-4002. For sales inquiries and reseller information, including discounts, bulk sales, customized editions, and premium sales, please contact our Customer Care department at 800-434-3422.

Manufactured in the United States of America

5   4   3   2   1

# THE KAUFFMAN CENTER SERIES ON MANAGING GROWTH

What does it take to grow a company? The Kauffman Center for Entrepreneurial Leadership has identified three bodies of knowledge that entrepreneurs need to know "cold" in order to manage growth. They are as follows:

- How to build an awesome organization
- How to finance growth
- How to make the necessary leadership changes as their companies transform through growth

Few resources exist to help entrepreneurs master these critical areas, so the Kauffman Center and publisher Hungry Minds have joined to create a unique series of books to fill this information void. The mission of the Kauffman Center Series on Managing Growth is to enable entrepreneurs to manage and accelerate the growth of their companies.

Presented in a concise, lively format, the books in this series are designed to match the needs of busy entrepreneurs who are short on time and want quick access to ideas that will help them build stronger organizations. Key points are augmented by stories from successful entrepreneurs, by boxes highlighting vital signs, by red flags indicating problems that need action, and by keys to success.

*Leading at the Speed of Growth* is the first book in the Kauffman Center Series on Managing Growth. Watch for others to come. Each is a major building block in any entrepreneur's knowledge base of how to grow a successful company. For a schedule of when new books will appear, visit www.entreworld.org or www.hungryminds.com.

# MISSION

The mission of *Leading at the Speed of Growth* is to enable many more entrepreneurs to be great leaders of growth companies.

# ABOUT THE AUTHORS

## KATHERINE CATLIN

For the past 15 years, Katherine Catlin has helped CEOs and their executive teams manage the challenges of fast-paced growth. As founding partner of The Catlin Group, a consulting firm in Hingham, Massachusetts that works with entrepreneurial companies nationwide, she created and leads High Growth CEO Forums, where CEOs regularly meet to exchange ideas, challenges, and best practices for growth. Catlin also developed Building the Profit Spiral™, a proven growth-planning process that enables CEOs not only to avoid typical pitfalls, but also to define winning strategies, build a cohesive management team, and gain companywide commitment to growth goals. Her firm has established a Web site for CEOs, www.ceoexchange.com, that provides ideas and information on growth issues.

## JANA MATTHEWS

In 1993 Jana Matthews left her own company and joined the Kauffman Center for Entrepreneurial Leadership as a senior program director. Since then, she's been busy figuring out what entrepreneurs need to know to manage growth. Working with the Young Entrepreneurs' Organization (YEO) and other successful entrepreneurs, she and her team have designed the Kauffman Gatherings of Entrepreneurs, as well as CD-ROMs, materials for Entreworld, Web casts, and other programs. Matthews has a doctorate from Harvard, has written several books, and has founded three companies, including Boulder Quantum Ventures. She enjoys writing books, helping entrepreneurs build successful companies, and fly-fishing in New Zealand.

# CONTENTS

# List of Illustrations

# FOREWORD

Ewing Marion Kauffman was a true entrepreneurial leader. Born into a modest home in Kansas City in 1916, he left as a young man to serve in the U.S. Navy. After returning to his hometown he took a job to provide for his family. He believed that hard work, dedication to principles, and respect for others formed the path to success. When he wasn't treated fairly by his employer, he quit.

With an initial investment of $5,000, Mr. Kauffman started a pharmaceutical company in the basement of his house in 1950. First-year sales reached $36,000 and the company made a net profit of $1,000. Over the years, he assembled a team and built Marion Laboratories, Inc., into a diversified healthcare colossus. In 1989, when it merged with Merrell Dow, Marion Laboratories had 3,200 employees, annual sales of approximately $1 billion, and a value of more than $6 billion. The company operates today as part of Aventis, one of the world's leading life science companies focused on pharmaceuticals and agriculture. Aventis has 90,000 employees worldwide and revenues of approximately $19 billion.

"Mr. K," as he was called, used his entrepreneurial skills to create several other successful organizations. For example, he brought major league baseball back to his community by purchasing the Kansas City Royals. In typical entrepreneurial fashion, Mr. K developed the Royals into a championship team that won six divisional titles, two American League pennants, and the 1985 World Series. Mr. K's Royals boosted the city's economic base, profile, and civic pride. He also created the Ewing Marion Kauffman Foundation as an "uncommon philanthropy" and endowed it with over $1 billion.

In 1992, a year before his death, Mr. K created the Kauffman Center for Entrepreneurial Leadership at the Kauffman Foundation. He recognized that the health of our economy is dependent on the ability of entrepreneurs to grow companies and was convinced that the best way to help entrepreneurs is to identify and teach the knowledge, skills, and values that contribute to entrepreneurial success. If entrepreneurs could learn how to develop successful companies, jobs would be created and the economy would be strengthened. This, he believed, would help the Kauffman Foundation achieve its mission of "self-sufficient people in healthy communities."

The Kauffman Center for Entrepreneurial Leadership is the largest organization in the world with the sole purpose of encouraging entrepreneurial success at all ages and levels, from elementary-school students to entrepreneurs leading high-growth companies.

Mr. Kauffman is one of those few founding entrepreneurs who stayed with his company for more than 40 years. His ability to learn from experiences and his reflections about what's required to be a successful entrepreneur have provided us with a rich legacy of knowledge about entrepreneurial leadership, the importance of continual learning, and the spirit of discovery. This book is a distillation of what we have learned from him—and from many other successful entrepreneurs—about the transitions they and their companies have had to make to be successful.

This book is the first in a series and one of a wide range of learning resources created by the Kauffman Center for entrepreneurs. In addition to books, the Center offers Kauffman Gatherings of Entrepreneurs, www.entreworld.org, diagnostic surveys to identify "what you know and what you don't know you don't know," the Kauffman Business EKG online benchmarking system, CD-ROMs, audiotapes, and other products and services—all designed to help entrepreneurs pilot their companies through growth. These resources have been developed by and with hundreds of successful entrepreneurs who have shared their knowledge, insights, and stories so that others might learn from them. We hope you find them useful as you work to write your own entrepreneurial success story.

*Katherine Catlin, Partner*
*The Catlin Group*


*Jana Matthews, President*
*Boulder Quantum Ventures*
*High Growth Expert*
*Kauffman Center for Entrepreneurial Leadership*

# ACKNOWLEDGMENTS

Over the past few years, we've worked with hundreds of remarkable entrepreneurial leaders. Their willingness to talk about their experiences, and share personal insights and lessons learned has enabled us to discover the critical stages and challenges of growth. The Kauffman Center's Gatherings of Entrepreneurs, The Catlin Group's High Growth CEO Forums, our own consulting projects, workshops for software and Internet councils, and in-depth discussions with entrepreneurs have provided many opportunities for us to learn about the evolution of growth companies. The leadership changes required to meet the challenges of growth are especially significant. We thank all these entrepreneurs for sharing their knowledge and experiences, and for helping us help other entrepreneurs.

We also want to thank our families, in particular Chip and Chuck. They believed in us and encouraged us at every step along the way. Likewise, we want to acknowledge the support we have received from Brad Feld, as well as Kate Pope Hodel, John Tyler, and other colleagues at the Kauffman Center. We also want to thank members of The Catlin Group, as well as Jeanne Yocum, Tom Phillips, Michael Warshaw, Judy Farren, and Pat Mullaly for all their help. Finally, we want to acknowledge the contributions of our agent, Jim Levine, as well as Mark Butler and the team at Hungry Minds. They have helped us bring this book from a dream to reality.

# CHAPTER 1

# THE CHALLENGE
# OF GROWTH

**Your company is your idea, your risk, and your life. You are the leader. But as it grows, it needs to change; and your role must evolve to match those changes. Your challenge is to become the dynamic leader that your company needs through *every* stage of its growth.**

In the last decade, entrepreneurship has exploded in America. Ambitious individuals—people like you, who have a dream—are taking control of their own destinies, seizing opportunities, capturing new markets, and creating new wealth for themselves and the managers and employees they lead.

But the sad reality is that relatively few members of this wave of entrepreneurs will still be in charge when the companies they founded break through to super success.

Some people deliberately choose to be "serial entrepreneurs," starting and selling or leaving one firm after another because the Start-up and early stages of a business are what they enjoy most. But many other business founders who do want to stay with their companies fail to achieve their visions of growth, and others are forced out because investors doubt their ability to transform themselves from an entrepreneur to the CEO of a large, high-growth organization.

Why is this? Why are people like Bill Gates of Microsoft, Michael Dell of Dell Computers, Anita Roddick of The Body Shop, and Richard Branson of Virgin Atlantic the exceptions—founders who remain firmly at the helm as their companies soar to extraordinary heights? We believe such leaders succeed because they are able to transform their leadership roles and styles as their companies grow. As Charles Darwin taught us, it's not how fast or smart you are, but your ability to adapt that determines whether you survive.

The irony of entrepreneurial leadership is that the very behaviors and habit patterns that lead to success at one stage of growth can contribute to failure in the next stage. It seems that just when you get good at something, you discover it's the wrong thing to be doing! It's important to understand and learn about the different kinds of knowledge and skills that are needed in each stage of your company's growth and development.

How can you learn to make the right changes in your leadership style at the right time? Begin with this book. It explains how to lead a company through growth, once you've survived the Start-up stage. In the book, we describe in detail the following aspects of growth:

- The three distinct stages of growth—*Initial Growth, Rapid Growth,* and *Continuous Growth*—that mark an organization's evolution after it has passed through the Start-up stage and has stabilized into a "real" company

- The "red flags" that signal the advent of a new stage in your company's evolution and that demand changes in your leadership to ensure continued success

- Your changing role and the key responsibilities you must assume if you are going to remain an entrepreneurial leader as your company grows through each stage of development

- The habits you must break and the personal transitions—specific changes in behavior and leadership style—you need to make to successfully take on each new role, growing from a founding entrepreneur into a great entrepreneurial CEO

- A planning model called Building the Profit Spiral™ that will help you foster the growth of your company

This book is full of stories about entrepreneurs who have faced the same issues you are facing—men and women who have made the journey from entrepreneur to CEO. Their companies range in size from 10 to 800 employees and from $1 million to $150 million in revenue. We've provided the context and then organized their stories to illustrate the points. Some of the entrepreneurs were not willing to share their confidential stories and candid insights if they had to name names of people and companies, so the quotes are anonymous. We've selected the best stories from entrepreneurs who are role models, those people who have led their organizations out of Start-up and through the other various stages of growth. All of them know what it's like to experience significant annual growth of 20 percent, 50 percent, or more. From these successful founding entrepreneurs, you can learn what it takes to manage growth and achieve true entrepreneurial success.

Like you, these entrepreneurial leaders began with an intuitive leadership style. In the early stages of your company, you ride the Start-up wave, put out fires, and make decisions on the fly. In this Start-up phase, your business is still new enough, and generally small enough, for you to manage all its needs on a day-to-day basis and to improvise as needed. You know all the jobs to be done, make all the decisions, work from a plan that's more-or-less developing in your head as you go along, and make changes as opportunities present themselves.

In other words, you operate in a do-it-yourself mode. You are the Doer and the Decision Maker.

But once the company begins to grow beyond this Start-up stage, you must alter your style from seat-of-the-pants, intuitive leadership to a more deliberate approach: growth by design. Yet even as your company reaches new stages of growth and you shift roles, you need to retain the best of your entrepreneurial characteristics and lead with consistent goals. That's one tall order, calling on you to continually accomplish these tasks:

- Develop markets, products/services, customers, and strategies to win.

- Develop internal processes for planning, management and work flow, as well as the infrastructure to sustain expansion and growth.

- Develop teams and people to perform the tasks that produce exceptional results.

- Develop the cultural environment so that it aligns and motivates those teams and people to work together as effectively as possible.

- Finally, and perhaps most difficult, monitor the evolution of your company and change your leadership style to match its current stage of growth.

None of these tasks will be easy. You will face challenging personal transitions. But since the ability to change grows with learning, constant learning is the most critical behavior you need to develop.

The good news is that you may already have what it takes to transform yourself into a highly successful entrepreneurial CEO. The Classic Entrepreneurial Strengths (see box) provide the strong foundation you need, no matter which stage of growth your company is experiencing.

## VITAL SIGNS: CLASSIC ENTREPRENEURIAL STRENGTHS

- Visionary and pioneering

- Great at seeing possibilities where others don't

- Always searching for new opportunities and challenges

- Passionate and energetic

- Driven to achieve results with high standards of excellence

- Creative and innovative idea generators; thinking "out of the box"

- Always striving to do things better

- Proactive and future-focused

- Smart, capable, and decisive

- Driven by a sense of urgency

- Confident about risk-taking

- Problem solvers who love new challenges and believe nothing is impossible

- Determined to create wealth, for themselves and others, and make a difference

But in order to transform into a truly great entrepreneurial leader of a high-growth company, you'll need to keep practicing all the Classic Entrepreneurial Strengths *plus* learn how to:

- Plan, including balancing short-term and long-term goals of all constituencies.

- Communicate to produce alignment.

- Build your entrepreneurial team and facilitate their working as a team.

- Resolve conflicts.

- Understand that people and culture are your key assets.

- Learn from every success and failure you have and from mentors and other successful entrepreneurs.

As you move through the stages of growth and add new roles and responsibilities, the creativity, drive, and will to succeed that made you an entrepreneur in the first place will enable you to take on the new leadership roles and responsibilities that are necessary to propel the growth of your company. Your ability to do this creates a powerful and even unbeatable competitive advantage. You have experience, insights, and attitudes that are generally lacking in CEOs who have never started a company from scratch. These attributes make you better prepared to deal with the tough challenges that come your way as the CEO of a growing company operating in a highly competitive business environment. In short, you have what it takes to succeed *if* you are willing to grow, change, and assume new sets of roles and responsibilities as the company moves through the various stages of growth.

As your business grows, your new roles and responsibilities will require new knowledge and skills. Sometimes you will simply apply what you already know to new situations, but other times you will have to learn new things and add new skills to your repertoire. This book will show you what you need to know and how your roles and responsibilities will change as the company grows.

At the beginning of this chapter, we mentioned the three stages of growth that follow Start-up. As you learn more about these stages, bear in mind that growth is a continuum that companies move through at different speeds. For example, the transition from Initial Growth to Rapid Growth can happen very quickly, and the two stages may seem to overlap for a time, especially in a fast-paced industry. Sometimes, different units of the company can be in different stages, as well. Defining precisely where you are on the growth continuum at any given moment is less important than knowing the types of changes you should expect in order to become the leader your company needs.

In your hands is a book that can guide you through the transitions you will have to make if you want to pilot your company through this continuum of growth and onward to exceptional heights. Throughout this book you'll learn from their own words how other entrepreneurs figured out the secrets of successful leadership and sustained growth.

FOR A LONG TIME AFTER I STARTED MY COMPANY, I MADE EVERY DECISION. I WAS THE ONLY REAL EXPERT, SO I ENDED UP TEACHING EVERYONE I HIRED ALL ABOUT IT. I ALSO HAD AN EGO, SO I FELT I COULD MAKE BETTER DECISIONS THAN ANYONE ELSE. I ENDED UP BEING AN ILL-INFORMED, UNEDUCATED DICTATOR. IT WAS VERY HARD TO GET PAST THAT STAGE. IN HINDSIGHT, I SEE HOW IT HELD EVERYTHING BACK. WE WEREN'T ABLE TO REALLY GROW UNTIL I WAS ABLE TO CHANGE MY LEADERSHIP STYLE. I WISH I'D FIGURED THAT OUT SOONER.

ESPECIALLY IN THOSE INITIAL STAGES, WHEN YOU'RE WORKING SO HARD, IT SEEMS LIKE THERE'S NO TIME TO SEEK OUT ADVICE FROM OTHERS. YOU'RE TOO BUSY TRYING TO STAY FOCUSED ON DOING THE RIGHT THINGS IN THE MIDST OF ALL THE STUFF THAT'S GOING ON AROUND YOU. BUT IT'S REALLY IMPORTANT TO MAKE SURE YOU'RE ALWAYS LEARNING. THE BEST WAY TO DO THAT IS TO GET PLENTY OF INPUT FROM OUTSIDERS, LIKE CUSTOMERS, MEMBERS OF YOUR BOARD, AND ANALYSTS. LISTEN AND LEARN FROM THEM, EVEN IF—ESPECIALLY IF—THEY'RE CRITICAL OF WHAT YOU DO.

YOU DON'T EVER CHANGE WHO YOU ARE, NOT REALLY. WHAT YOU DO CHANGE ARE SOME OF THE ROLES YOU PLAY. THE WAY I LOOK AT IT IS THAT MY JOB CHANGES, BUT I DON'T. PEOPLE ALWAYS KNOW WHO I AM AND WHAT I STAND FOR. YET, AS MY COMPANY GREW, MY ROLE HAD TO KEEP CHANGING, FROM CHEERLEADER TO EGO FEEDER AND SO FORTH. WHEN WE HAD 15 PEOPLE, I WAS THE DOER AND LEADER. NOW THAT WE HAVE 100 PEOPLE, I HAVE TO BE MUCH LESS OF THE DAY-TO-DAY DECISION MAKER AND MORE A LEADER OF LEADERS. IT'S BEEN A REAL EDUCATION PROCESS FOR ME.

ONE OF THE THINGS I WISH I HAD KNOWN THAT SCREWED US UP IN THE EARLY YEARS IS THE IMPORTANCE OF UNDERSTANDING WHAT YOUR PERSONAL GOAL IS. WHAT ARE YOU TRYING TO DO WITH THE COMPANY? THEN MAKE SURE THAT ALL YOUR SYSTEMS AND ALL THE THINGS YOU'RE DOING IN THE COMPANY REFLECT WHAT YOUR PERSONAL GOALS ARE OR WHAT THE PURPOSE OF THE COMPANY IS.

FOR INSTANCE, ONE GOAL MIGHT BE QUICK PROFITS, MAKING SOME MONEY TO DO SOMETHING. ANOTHER MIGHT BE CASH FLOW AND PERSONAL INCOME. SOME PEOPLE ARE INTERESTED IN RUNNING THEIR COMPANY FOR A LONG TIME, REALLY JUST TO PRODUCE A GOOD STANDARD OF LIVING FOR THEM-SELVES. OTHERS ARE LOOKING FOR CAPITAL GAINS FOR GROWING AND SELL-ING. THEY REALLY WANT TO BUILD SOMETHING, GROW IT, SELL IT, AND MOVE ON TO THE NEXT THING.

THERE'S ANOTHER SET OF ENTREPRENEURS WHO ARE INTERESTED IN BUILDING SUSTAINABLE ORGANIZATIONS THAT WILL LAST A LONG TIME. THEY ARE INTERESTED IN BUILDING THE NEXT HEWLETT-PACKARD, THE NEXT MICROSOFT. THAT TAKES A VERY DIFFERENT APPROACH TO LEADERSHIP.

ANOTHER GOAL MIGHT BE TO DO SOMETHING USEFUL. THE FINANCIAL PART ISN'T A KEY DRIVER FOR THEM. OTHER ENTREPRENEURS ARE INTERESTED IN THE PEOPLE ASPECTS OF BUILDING AN ORGANIZATION AND HAVING A PLACE WHERE PEOPLE ARE ALL VERY HAPPY.

HOW YOU LEAD YOUR COMPANY SHOULD REALLY DEPEND ON YOUR GOALS. KNOWING YOUR ANSWERS TO THESE QUESTIONS HELPS YOU DETERMINE THE DESIGN OF THE ORGANIZATION, AND SET UP YOUR COMPENSATION SYSTEMS, YOUR REWARD SYSTEMS, AND YOUR CULTURE. HAVING ALL THOSE IN ALIGN-MENT IS REALLY IMPORTANT.

# THIS BOOK IS YOUR MAP

In a sense, this book provides you with a map of the journey from entrepreneur to CEO. Remember what happened after Lewis and Clark mapped the territory west of the Mississippi? Thousands of pioneers traveled west because they had a map to follow. We want all our readers to use this book as a guide and to lead their companies through the stages of growth to success.

In this book, we highlight three stages of growth following Start-up: Initial Growth, Rapid Growth, and Continuous Growth.

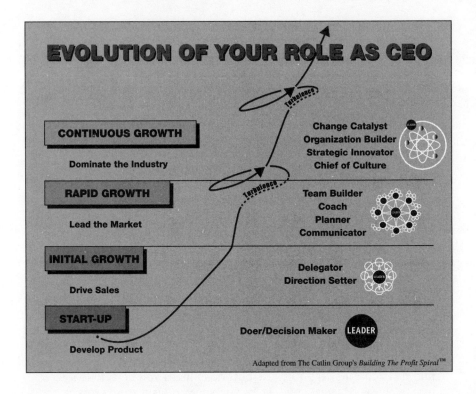

EVOLUTION OF YOUR ROLE AS CEO

**CONTINUOUS GROWTH**

Dominate the Industry

**RAPID GROWTH**

Lead the Market

**INITIAL GROWTH**

Drive Sales

**START-UP**

Develop Product

Change Catalyst
Organization Builder
Strategic Innovator
Chief of Culture

Team Builder
Coach
Planner
Communicator

Delegator
Direction Setter

Doer/Decision Maker  LEADER

Adapted from The Catlin Group's *Building The Profit Spiral*™

During Start-up you're trying to figure out what product or service to offer that will meet the needs of the market and ways your company can provide value to its customers.

**Initial Growth.** In this stage, your company is very sales driven as it tries to launch a new or different product, capture market share, and grow revenues. Company operations are fast paced, highly flexible, even chaotic. People do whatever is necessary to be successful.

**Rapid Growth.** In the second stage, your company is trying to achieve widespread use of its products or services, gain a significant share of its chosen markets, ward off advances from competitors, and move into a market leadership position. Lots of new people need to be hired—rounds and rounds of them. Integrating them and aligning their efforts can be a daunting, never-ending task.

**Continuous Growth.** This final stage comprises successive rounds of turbulence and periodic "reinventions" of the company. Rapid Growth has led to many more customers and market opportunities, a much larger employee base, a more complex organization, and the potential to dominate the industry. But more of everything also includes more potential to go out of control.

In Continuous Growth, the company tries to dominate the industry by finding new markets and growing new niches in the current market, expanding the product lines, providing more "total solutions" to help customers, and branding itself and its people as "thought leaders." Growth strategies include new product development, strategic alliances, acquisitions and mergers, spinning off subsidiaries, corporate partnerships to provide funding, and even an initial public offering (IPO).

But as the company changes, so do your roles and responsibilities. You'll need to make those changes in order to successfully lead your company through the stages of growth shown in the preceding figure, "Evolution of Your Role as CEO."

**INITIAL GROWTH**

**Delegator**
**Direction Setter**

# CHAPTER 2

# INITIAL GROWTH

**Leadership is knowing what you want, planning for it, and doing it as best you can. The first year of my company was the most intense time of my life, and I spent it in a constant sweat, worrying that I was making decisions too fast, too much on the fly. Yet as we grew and I was able to pull up a little, I could look back and see that although I certainly made some calls I would change in hindsight, I did pretty well overall. Most of my decisions were consistent with my goals. So when we started to grow, I was ready. And the company was ready. I know that's because I sat down before we started up and worked out exactly what I wanted to happen and what I could do to make it happen. I wasn't able to predict everything, that's for sure, but I went into it with a mindset that was clear and that I was able to lean on when it came to making quick, hard decisions about the company.**

## YOUR COMPANY'S NEW GOALS IN INITIAL GROWTH

In the beginning, your goal was to get started, recruit a few people, get some customers, generate some revenues, and keep afloat. You were busy figuring out what product or service to offer and which customers would want to buy it (see the following figure).

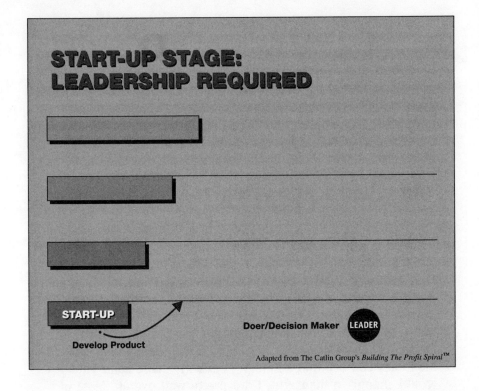

Adapted from The Catlin Group's *Building The Profit Spiral*™

But as you move into Initial Growth, your company's goals change from survival to development. In order to help your company succeed in Initial Growth, you must focus the company on the following:

- Developing and launching a great new product or service into the market.

- Being noticed for offering something different.

- Gaining visibility by winning over some impressive customers, which helps convince more and more customers to try your product.

- Trying to capture market share.

- Growing revenues.

In this stage, the company tends to be very sales driven. Company operations are fast paced, highly flexible, and often chaotic, as people experiment with new ideas, stay close to customers, and do whatever it takes to grab opportunities for increasing sales. This is a time for putting all the pieces together, positioning for competitive advantage, and building your company's ability to deliver (see the following figure).

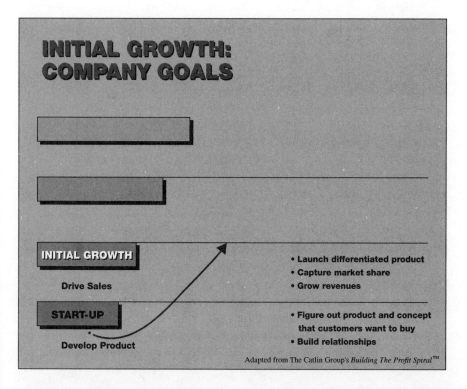

## INITIAL GROWTH: COMPANY GOALS

**INITIAL GROWTH**

Drive Sales

• Launch differentiated product
• Capture market share
• Grow revenues

**START-UP**

Develop Product

• Figure out product and concept
  that customers want to buy
• Build relationships

Adapted from The Catlin Group's *Building The Profit Spiral*™

## RED FLAGS: WARNING SIGNS THAT TELL YOU IT'S TIME TO CHANGE ROLES

All of a sudden, you start noticing some changes. These changes are indicators—red flags—that signal the movement of your company out of Start-up and into the Initial Growth stage. They signal that it's time to change your leadership role. Here are some red flags to watch out for:

 There's not enough time in the day. The people who want and need your time can't seem to get it.

*cont...*

*-continued*

 Even though you feel you're still the best person to make each decision in the business, it's becoming physically and emotionally impossible to do everything that needs to be done.

 Your bankers are asking financial questions you can't answer, and you're not sure you always have a good grip on where the money is going.

 Everyone seems to be constantly fighting fires. People who used to joke about how busy they were now complain that there's not enough time.

 You wake up worrying about operational tasks that someone else ought to be handling.

 All your customers want to meet with you, but finding the time to do so seems impossible for you.

 You see multiple new possibilities for growth, but you're not sure which ones to pursue.

 Managing all the risks alone feels like a burden.

 Suddenly you feel like you have a "real" company.

I LOOKED OUT MY DOOR ONE MORNING AND SAW EIGHT PEOPLE WAITING TO TALK TO ME. IT HIT ME THAT IT WAS TIME FOR ME TO GET SOME MIDDLE MANAGEMENT.

# YOUR ROLES AND KEY RESPONSIBILITIES

In the Start-up stage that preceded Initial Growth, you wore many hats as you took part in all the activities of the business. Essentially, you were in a "do-it-yourself" and "make-all-the-decisions-yourself" hands-on mode and enjoyed having the freedom to change your mind at any time. Your original vision and ideas drove the company forward.

You were clearly in charge with everyone, or just about everyone, reporting to you. Others may have made some decisions, but you had the last word and personally handled decisions of any significance. In the illustration at the beginning of the chapter, you were the whole circle.

However, as the company enters the Initial Growth stage, your leadership role must change from Doer and Decision Maker to Delegator and Direction Setter if you want the company to grow. The illustration that follows shows you, the leader, still in the middle of everything, but you must now begin to set up functional units within the company, then hire people to whom you delegate part of your roles and responsibilities.

Your role now is to decide where the company should be headed, delegate tasks to others so they can help you take the company there, then monitor progress on projects you've delegated to them. You can no longer do it all yourself, although you are still the ultimate decision maker for "big picture/big ticket" items (see the following figure).

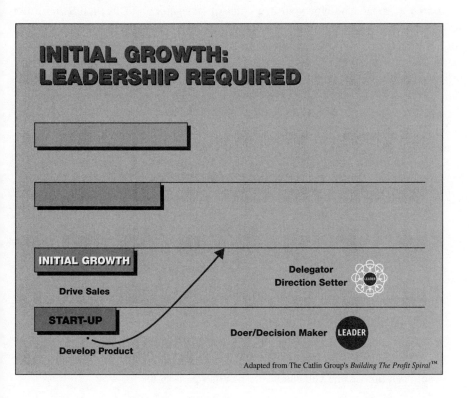

**INITIAL GROWTH: LEADERSHIP REQUIRED**

INITIAL GROWTH

Drive Sales

Delegator
Direction Setter

START-UP

Doer/Decision Maker    LEADER

Develop Product

Adapted from The Catlin Group's *Building The Profit Spiral*™

THE ROLE OF AN ENTREPRENEUR IS TO BE A MANAGER AND A LEADER AT THE SAME TIME. YOUR JOB IS TO TAKE THE COMPANY TO THE PLACE YOU SEE THAT IT NEEDS TO GO.

I HAVE NO PROBLEM WITH THE CONCEPT OF DELEGATION. I'M LAZY. I WANT TO DO AS LITTLE WORK AS POSSIBLE. SO I'M READY AND WILLING TO DELEGATE. BUT I HAVE HIGH STANDARDS THAT PEOPLE DON'T SEEM TO WANT TO MEET IN THE SAME WAY I DO. THAT'S MY DILEMMA. I HAD TO LEARN TO ENCOURAGE PEOPLE TO STRETCH, RECOGNIZING THAT AS THEY STRETCHED THEY MADE SOME MISTAKES. OF COURSE, LEARNING FROM THOSE MISTAKES IS KEY, AND CELEBRATING WHEN THE HIGH STANDARDS ARE MET! IT'S STILL HARD FOR ME, BUT I'VE GOTTEN BETTER AT TRUSTING THE PROCESS.

You need to understand how your new roles of Delegator and Direction Setter differ from your roles and responsibilities in Start-up. Then you were the center of everything. But in order to grow, you need to create an organization that's bigger than you, one that can sustain growth. This means you have to hire smart people, then delegate and trust them to manage so you can concentrate on the other things you need to put in place to promote your company's growth. But since the company is your creation, the extension of yourself and your values, you can't just let go.

Here's a checklist of things to do to prepare the company for Initial Growth and build the foundation for Rapid Growth:

- Articulate and reinforce your vision for the company as well as its high-growth opportunity and potential.

- Be conscious of your own personal values and goals for building the company. Define the game you want to play; set the direction, and then focus others on winning that game with your values.

- Find creative ways to do a lot with scarce resources. Encourage innovative experiments and ideas.

- Watch the critical performance indicators (especially cash flow and profitability), and use a sharp financial person to pay close attention to the business side of operations while you handle all the other parts of the job.

- Get input from customers, prospects, analysts, and investors and integrate these valuable outside perspectives into your own.

- Hire multitalented people whose values match yours. Aggressively find the people who really fit, both in skills and in values, and who will help grow the company. Don't hire the person who can do the job you have open right now; rather, hire people who can grow at least two levels as the company grows and your management structure becomes more sophisticated.

- Delegate responsibilities by establishing very clear goals and expectations for people. Then hold them accountable.

- Take advantage of mentors who have been through what you're about to experience. Join an organization such as the Young Entrepreneurs' Organization (YEO) or a CEO Forum so you can talk about your issues and learn from the experiences of other entrepreneurs.

THE FIRST YEARS OF MY COMPANY WERE LONELY TIMES FOR ME AND MY PARTNER BECAUSE WE DIDN'T KNOW ANYONE ELSE TRYING TO BUILD A COMPANY. WE REALLY THOUGHT THAT WE WERE THE FIRST ONES TO FACE THE PROBLEMS WE WERE HAVING TO DEAL WITH—HOW TO FORECAST REVENUE, WHEN TO HIRE NEW PEOPLE, AND HOW TO DELEGATE SO THAT WE WEREN'T THE ONLY ONES WHO COULD MAKE A DECISION. LUCKILY, I MET ANOTHER ENTREPRENEUR WHO INTRODUCED ME TO OTHER ENTREPRENEURS WHO WERE HAVING EXACTLY THE SAME PROBLEMS WE WERE. HE ALSO HELPED ME SET UP A BOARD OF ADVISORS. GETTING INVOLVED WITH A PEER GROUP AND SETTING UP A BOARD PROBABLY MADE THE DIFFERENCE BETWEEN FAILURE AND SUCCESS.

I BEGAN WITH A NONPAYING ADVISORY BOARD. I LOOKED FOR THOUGHT LEADERS AND LEADERS IN OTHER INDUSTRIES. IF I RAN INTO A REALLY SHARP CLIENT, I WOULD ASK HIM TO BE ON MY BOARD. ONCE I GOT THE FIRST COUPLE OF PEOPLE, THE NEXT ONES WERE EASIER, BUT I HAD TO BE PERSISTENT AND AGGRESSIVE TO GET THE PEOPLE I WANTED. THE BOARD REALLY HELPED ME. THE BEST THING THE BOARD DID WAS TO PROTECT ME FROM MYSELF. MANY TIMES, THEY ASKED ME JUST THE RIGHT QUESTION OR TOLD ME I WAS ABOUT TO MAKE A DUMB DECISION. THEY NEVER STOPPED ME FROM DOING ANYTHING, BUT THEY HELPED ME UNDERSTAND MY LIMITATIONS. AFTER A YEAR, IT BECAME A BOARD OF DIRECTORS. I WISH I HAD CREATED THE BOARD OF DIRECTORS EARLIER.

I DIDN'T DO THE HIRING I REALLY NEEDED TO DO UNTIL WE HIT THE WALL. WE WERE EXPERIENCING FAST GROWTH, AND WE WERE UNDERCAPITALIZED. I HIRED A LOT OF PEOPLE, AND IT GOT SCARY FOR A WHILE. IT SEEMED AS IF ALL I WAS DOING WITH MY TIME WAS TRAINING AND HANDHOLDING. AND IT TOOK ME A WHILE TO LEARN THAT DELEGATING IS NOT ABDICATING. YOU STILL HAVE OVERSIGHT AUTHORITY AND CONTROL, BUT YOU'RE PASSING PRIMARY RESPONSIBILITY ONTO OTHERS. I MADE THE MISTAKE ONCE OR TWICE OF DUMPING SOMETHING ON MY PEOPLE AND WALKING AWAY, WHICH FELT GOOD BUT CARRIES A VERY HIGH PRICE. BUT I LEARNED HOW TO WORK WITH THE PEOPLE I HIRE. IT TURNED OUT THAT OVERHIRING WAS ONE OF THE SMARTEST THINGS I DID. I WAS ABLE TO PASS ON A VISION I HAD FOR THE BUSINESS, THAT IT WAS GOING TO GET TO A CERTAIN POINT. WHEN WE GOT THERE, I REALIZED I HAD A LOT OF PEOPLE IN PLACE WHO WANTED A CAREER, NOT JUST A JOB. THEY ARE STILL WITH ME, STILL HAPPY AND MOTIVATED.

IF SOMEONE YOU'VE HIRED DOESN'T HAVE VALUES COMPATIBLE WITH THOSE OF THE COMPANY, GET THEM OUT, QUICKLY, ESPECIALLY IF THEY ARE MANAGERS WHO WILL BE INFLUENCING NEW HIRES. THIS IS VERY DIFFICULT TO DO IF THEY ARE REALLY GOOD AT THE JOB YOU NEED THEM TO PERFORM. BUT THIS IS A KEY LESSON I LEARNED THE HARD WAY. IT CAN MAKE OR BREAK YOUR COMPANY.

Initial Growth can be difficult to manage. Every step—adding employees and customers, as well as partnerships, investors, and other new constituencies—means new growing pains. As the complexity and scale of the company increase, you will experience some defining moments. You will realize that you can't do it all by yourself any more and that you don't know how to solve some of the more complex issues the company is facing.

IT TOOK TIME FOR ME TO LEARN THERE ARE SOME THINGS I DO WELL AND SOME THINGS I DO VERY POORLY. A FEW YEARS INTO THE BUSINESS, WE REALIZED WE NEEDED TO DIVERSIFY. WE MADE SOME CHANGES AND TOOK ON SOME UNGODLY OVERHEAD. I HAD TO STEP BACK AND REALIZE THAT I'M ACTUALLY A LOUSY MANAGER. IT WAS A REAL BLOW TO MY EGO, BUT THE BEST THING IN THE WORLD FOR MY COMPANY WAS WHEN I HAD TO ADMIT ALL THE THINGS I COULDN'T DO WELL. AS SOON AS I DID, I TURNED OVER THE PRESIDENCY TO SOMEONE ELSE AND FOCUSED ON WHAT I DO BEST. TODAY, WE'RE A BETTER COMPANY FOR IT.

If you continue to make all the decisions by yourself during Initial Growth, you will create a significant bottleneck that will negatively affect the company's ability to grow. New hires and/or promotions are crucial, especially at the management level. This means you must address:

- Issues of delegation and management of performance

- Development and communication of vision, values, and goals

- Establishment of clear new roles and expectations for the new hires

ONE DAY MY MENTOR SAID TO ME, "LOOK, THIS ISN'T WORKING. YOU'VE GOT TO PUT IN A MANAGEMENT STRUCTURE. YOU CAN'T HAVE EVERYBODY REPORTING TO YOU." THAT WASN'T OBVIOUS TO ME AS AN ENTREPRENEUR. BUT THINGS WERE GETTING CRAZY, SO, IN A RUSH, I HIRED SOME PEOPLE. AND MADE LOTS OF MISTAKES. I DIDN'T EVEN CHECK REFERENCES, AND I MADE SOME PRETTY BAD HIRES. SOMEONE SAID I NEEDED TO BRING IN SOME MANAGERS. I DIDN'T EVEN KNOW WHAT A MANAGER WAS. IN FACT, IN A LOT OF WAYS I'M STILL LEARNING WHAT A MANAGER IS. BUT WE DID BRING IN SOME MANAGERS. THAT WAS GREAT. THAT REALLY HELPED. IT ALLOWED US TO GROW.

# PERSONAL TRANSITIONS REQUIRED

To manage Initial Growth, an entrepreneur must make two major changes in roles and style: Give up some responsibilities and change from a reactive to a proactive style.

## GIVE UP SOME RESPONSIBILITIES

You must divide your job into components. Decide what to let go and what to keep. Delegating to others can be very difficult; it's easy to procrastinate because delegating requires you to take the time to share your knowledge and thinking with other people. But even though it seems much easier—and it is definitely quicker—to just do it yourself, it is critical that you take time to give direction to others. If you don't spin off parts of your job, the company won't be able to grow beyond your individual capacity. So, while still retaining the oversight and ultimate decision-making authority, you must turn over some responsibilities to others and guide them as they learn to handle these new tasks.

ALL MY MONEY, MY INVESTORS' MONEY, MY EMPLOYEES, AND MY REPUTATION
WERE ON THE LINE. I FELT HUGE PRESSURE FROM THAT RESPONSIBILITY. I FELT
I HAD TO PERSONALLY MANAGE ALL THE RISKS. I DIDN'T TRUST ANYONE ELSE
TO MAKE THE SHREWD BUSINESS DECISIONS I KNEW I COULD MAKE. BUT I WAS
BURNING OUT FAST AND HAD TO CHANGE. I REALIZED THAT ONE DAY WHEN MY
SON TOLD ME, "DAD, YOU'RE WORKING 24/7. HOW CAN YOU KEEP IT UP?" SO
I HIRED A SEARCH FIRM AND QUICKLY BUT CAREFULLY BROUGHT IN SOME VERY
SENIOR MANAGERS, PEOPLE I FELT I COULD TRUST. THAT ALLOWED US TO CON-
TINUE OUR EXPLOSIVE GROWTH, AND IT ALLOWED ME TO BE A MUCH BETTER
LEADER.

As your company begins to grow, there are changes you must make in your own
behavior:

- **Stop making all the decisions, solving all the problems, and answering all
the questions.** Instead, you must consciously define which decisions should be
made by others, and turn requests back to the people who need to make these
decisions. Help them discover their own capabilities while giving them the freedom *not* to have to come to you for everything. It may be especially frustrating
when you feel you can do the job better and with more creativity and energy
than they will. After all, you've done it your way until now and you've been
very successful! But while it may seem counterintuitive, you actually gain, not
lose, control when you delegate and monitor performance.

    THE BEST THING I EVER DID WITH MY COMPANY WAS TO RESTRUCTURE
    IN A WAY THAT ALLOWS ME TO FOCUS MORE ON CREATING NEW PROD-
    UCTS AND LESS ON THE DAY-TO-DAY ADMINISTRATIVE STUFF.

    I HAVE A SIGN ON MY DESK THAT REMINDS ME TO ASK THE QUESTIONS
    RATHER THAN AUTOMATICALLY PROVIDE ALL THE ANSWERS.

- **Put your trust in other people.** Allow them to develop their skills and be
accountable for producing the results you both agree are important. You can
mitigate risks by delegating to people whom you truly believe are smarter,
faster, better than you are in their fields of expertise. Then you need to hold
them accountable—if not for the entire decision, then for a portion of it, or for
a proposal that you approve. Many entrepreneurs who have done so have been
pleasantly surprised when people came up with ideas and ways of doing things
they never thought of themselves.

> HIRING GOOD PEOPLE AND TRAINING THEM IS MY MOST IMPORTANT
> SKILL. I TRY TO TRAIN PEOPLE TO REPLACE ME, SO I CAN LET THEM
> LOOSE TO MANAGE THE REST OF THE ORGANIZATION. MY PHILOSOPHY
> IS THAT IF SOMETHING *CAN* BE DELEGATED, IT *MUST* BE DELEGATED.
> THE BIGGER MY BUSINESS GETS, THE MORE I NEED PEOPLE WHO CAN
> TAKE OVER THE DAY-TO-DAY TASKS SO I CAN FOCUS ON LONG-TERM
> STRATEGY.

- **Make an effort to recognize others, give credit to your people, and share the limelight.** Credit is usually given to the person in the room with the biggest title or the most authority. Since people will give you the credit for the company's positive performance, you'll need to learn to deflect the credit and thank appropriate staff members for their ideas, actions, and the results they produce.

> AS A LEADER YOU HAVE TO BE WILLING TO SHARE THE CREDIT. I HAD TO
> LEARN THAT PEOPLE COME TO WORK FOR MANY REASONS, NOT JUST A
> PAYCHECK. IN THE BEGINNING, I THOUGHT THE ANSWER WAS ALWAYS
> TO THROW MORE MONEY INTO THE SITUATION. I WAS WRONG. MONEY
> IS AN ISSUE, BUT IF PEOPLE ARE PAID ENOUGH, IT IS USUALLY THEIR
> THIRD OR FOURTH PRIORITY. AFTER FOOD, CLOTHING, AND SHELTER, THE
> GREATEST HUMAN NEED IS RECOGNITION. YOU CAN GET A LOT MORE
> MILEAGE OUT OF RECOGNITION AND SPECIAL AWARDS THAN YOU CAN
> WITH MONEY. NOW I TRY TO PROVIDE MY EMPLOYEES WITH OWNERSHIP
> OF THEIR WORK, OPPORTUNITY, AND PERSONAL GROWTH. I TRY TO
> CREATE AN ENVIRONMENT IN WHICH INDIVIDUALS CAN REACH A PRO-
> FESSIONAL LEVEL THEY NEVER DREAMED WAS POSSIBLE.

Sharing responsibilities through effective delegation is critical. Monitoring the performance of those to whom you have delegated enables you to praise them for their successes or redirect their activities if they are off-course. If you fail to delegate, you risk becoming an authoritarian micromanager and your people will be demotivated because they perceive you don't trust them. But failing to recognize people's contributions will also demotivate them. The result will be people who quit or quit trying to make a difference and sit around waiting for you to make all the decisions. Be careful not to fall into the "founder's trap," or the company will not be able to grow beyond your own mental and physical capacities; and that limitation will severely restrict its potential.

## CHANGE FROM A REACTIVE TO A PROACTIVE STYLE

The wildly opportunistic, sales-driven, "We can do whatever paying customers want" operational style that enabled the company to survive the Start-up stage and created its original success is not sustainable and will not lead to continued growth. Proactive planning that sets a direction for the future is critical. Consciously choose the target markets and the types of customers that will stimulate the best growth.

NEVER PROCRASTINATE ON IMPORTANT DECISIONS. GATHER INFORMATION FROM EVERYONE, BUT MAKE THE BIG STRATEGIC DECISIONS YOURSELF. MAKE THEM FAST. DON'T COMPROMISE YOUR VALUES. FOLLOW YOUR INSTINCTS. YOU HAVE TO FILTER ALL THE ADVICE YOU GET. YOU CAN'T LISTEN TO IT ALL BECAUSE IT CAN THROW YOU OFF FROM WHAT YOU'RE TRYING TO ACCOMPLISH. LET YOUR BANKERS AND CPAS, AND SOMETIMES EVEN YOUR EMPLOYEES, ADAPT TO WHAT YOU'RE DOING; NOT VICE VERSA.

You also need to make choices about what to do and what not to do to achieve the focus and direction needed to move to the next level of growth. You must create and communicate a concrete vision and strategy for growth that identifies specific aspects of the company you want to develop within two to three years, complete with action steps and a description of the organization that will take you there.

IT'S NOT ENOUGH JUST TO BE ABLE TO FOCUS. YOU HAVE TO BE ABLE TO FOCUS ON THE RIGHT THINGS, LIKE THE VISION AND GOALS FOR THE COMPANY, THE THINGS FROM WHICH ALL OTHER DECISIONS FLOW.

IT WAS ONLY WHEN WE SAID NO TO SOME NEW BUSINESS OPPORTUNITIES THAT WE REALIZED WE HAD A REAL FOCUS AND A REAL STRATEGY.

# HABITS TO BREAK

In order to make a successful transition from your role as Doer and Decision Maker in Start-up to Delegator and Direction Setter in the Initial Growth stage, you must break three habits that are typical of start-up entrepreneurs: shooting from the hip, resisting structure, and resisting the development of processes.

## SHOOTING FROM THE HIP

Working without a plan and chasing every new opportunity that comes along are signs that you are shooting from the hip. You cannot lead unless your people trust you, and they won't trust you if they believe you're a shoot-from-the-hip cowboy. You won't be able to sustain growth, your people will get confused about what they are supposed to do, and they will resent having to change priorities daily. The net result will be delay and a dangerous loss of focus.

IN THE BEGINNING, I WAS THE COMPANY. WE ONLY HAD THREE EMPLOYEES, AND I DID EVERYTHING, INCLUDING THE BOOKS, AND MADE ALL THE DECISIONS RIGHT DOWN TO THE COFFEE SERVICE. BUT YOU HAVE TO GRADUALLY LET GO OF THAT IF YOU EVER WANT TO REACH THE NEXT STAGE. YOU HAVE TO FOCUS ON THE KEY ARTERIES OF THE BUSINESS: ACCESS TO CASH, PEOPLE, PERSISTENCE, AND, MOST OF ALL, A PLAN. YOU SET THE VISION AND YOU CRAFT THE PLAN. THAT'S WHAT A LEADER DOES.

## RESISTING STRUCTURE

Although some entrepreneurs resist structure because they fear it will inhibit creativity, establishing an organizational structure with clearly delineated roles and responsibilities actually promotes creativity rather than stifling it. A plan and a structure can liberate, rather than constrain, you. When people know what the plan and focus are, and they are asked to find creative ways to achieve the plan, they will produce a lot of new ideas and solutions.

WHEN I THINK OF MY BUSINESS, I DIVIDE IT INTO TWO PIECES: THE ECONOMIC ENGINE AND THE ORGANIZATION. THAT'S HOW WE ORIENT OUR PLANNING. THE CLASSIC MISTAKE ENTREPRENEURS MAKE IS TO THINK ABOUT THE ECONOMIC ENGINE AND FORGET THE ORGANIZATION. THEY FOCUS ON THE BUSINESS AND NOT SO MUCH ON THE INFRASTRUCTURE, PEOPLE, MANAGEMENT, AND ORGANIZATION SIDE OF THINGS. YET THE SUCCESS OF THE ECONOMIC ENGINE, ITS ENERGY AND POWER, COMES DIRECTLY FROM THE WORK YOU DO ON ESTABLISHING STRUCTURE AND SETTING UP THE ORGANIZATION.

## RESISTING THE DEVELOPMENT OF PROCESSES

Too many entrepreneurs think that developing formalized processes and standard operating procedures will stifle the innovation and flexibility that are critical to maintaining the company's competitive edge and ability to grow. They are afraid those processes will turn the company into a rigid bureaucracy with red tape that imposes limitations and restricts people too much. But the opposite is true. Very few people like to spend time reinventing the wheel, and they hate to spin their wheels. Standard operating processes and procedures provide employees with a common set of responses for repetitive situations and allow them to save their energy and creativity for new challenges.

A LOT OF ENTREPRENEURS LIKE ME CAME OUT OF LARGE CORPORATIONS THAT WERE BUREAUCRATIC ORGANIZATIONS, AND WE'RE SCARED OF CREATING A SIMILAR ENVIRONMENT. BUT WE ENTREPRENEURS NEED TO UNDERSTAND THAT THERE IS A DIFFERENCE BETWEEN PLANNING AND CREATING A BUREAUCRACY. IT TOOK A WHILE FOR ME TO REALIZE THAT EVERYONE WASN'T GETTING IT LIKE I THOUGHT THEY WERE. LEARNING TO PLAN WAS KEY FOR US.

PART OF SETTING GOALS TOGETHER IS GIVING THE MANAGEMENT TEAM A SENSE OF RESPONSIBILITY FOR THE FINANCIALS. I'M STILL WORKING ON THIS, BUT WHAT HAS HELPED THE MOST HAS BEEN TEACHING THE MANAGERS ABOUT CASH FLOW AND MAXIMUM SUSTAINABLE GROWTH. NOW THEY KNOW THAT GROWTH IS CONTROLLED BY A NUMBER OF VARIABLES AND THAT THEY MUST ALWAYS BE IN EQUILIBRIUM.

WE'VE LEARNED THE IMPORTANCE OF REGULAR MEETINGS: TO STAY FOCUSED AND INFORMED. WE HAVE A WEEKLY "RESULTS MEETING" WITH THE MANAGERS AND OUR EMPLOYEE ADVISORY COMMITTEE, AND WE EVALUATE THE PROCESS OF THE MEETING AT THE END. WE RATE (FROM 1 TO 5) THREE AREAS: RESULTS ACCOMPLISHED; EFFECTIVENESS OF THE MEETING'S PROCESS; INDIVIDUALS' SATISFACTION WITH THEIR OWN CONTRIBUTION. WE REPORT FINANCIALS IN THE FIRST 12 MINUTES OR SO AND THEN THE REST OF THE TIME IS TO WORK ON PREDETERMINED AGENDA ITEMS.

I USED TO MAKE EVERY DECISION ON THE FLY WHEN WE WERE SMALLER, BUT I MADE A LOT OF MISTAKES THAT WAY. NOW I BELIEVE IN SETTING GOALS. I SIT DOWN WITH MY PEOPLE AND SAY, "LET'S FIGURE OUT WHAT YOU WANT FIRST, THEN WHAT I WANT, AND COME UP WITH A PLAN—A SET OF GOALS THAT WE WILL BOTH TRY TO DO IN THE COMING YEAR." WE FORMALIZE IT AND PUT IT IN WRITING. THE PROCESS IS VERY EMPOWERING, AND I DON'T THINK WE COULD HAVE EVER GROWN AS MUCH AS WE DID IF WE DIDN'T HAVE THESE PLANS.

Plans help create the future you want by pointing everyone in the right direction. You need to have just enough structure so people know what's expected and can identify and solve the right problems. Setting priorities through an accepted planning process achieves "buy-in" much better than the "idea-of-the-moment" or "strategy-du-jour" style that entrepreneurs often employ. Changes can and should be made to the plan you develop, but they need to be well considered as true opportunities that fit the fundamental market need, vision, and goals of the company.

ULTIMATELY, I AM NOT JUST RESPONSIBLE FOR THE PLAN, BUT ALSO FOR THE DECISIONS THAT WE SOMETIMES HAVE TO MAKE TO CHANGE THE PLAN. YOU KNOW WHAT THEY SAY: "LIFE IS WHAT HAPPENS TO YOU WHILE YOU'RE MAKING OTHER PLANS." SO WE'RE ALWAYS PREPARED TO AMEND OUR PLANS. BUT EVEN THOUGH PLANS CHANGE, WE WOULD NEVER BE ABLE TO MAKE DECISIONS IF WE DIDN'T CRAFT THOSE PLANS IN THE FIRST PLACE.

If you do not consciously break these habits of shooting from the hip and resisting structure and the development of processes—habits that are considered stereotypical of entrepreneurs—you will remain in the overly reactive style. What's worse, you could easily derail the company. Without a clear, written plan, people lose focus on what the company is trying to do. They pay attention to what seems most urgent as opposed to what may actually be most important. They complain about being confused by too many priorities, and they say they "don't have time" to consider new ideas or opportunities. They start burning out and asking, "Where is this company going anyway?" and "Do I really care?" If you don't communicate your vision, mission, and plans, and develop processes that enable your people to have input, they will perceive your decisions as capricious and seat-of-the-pants. The result will be scattered effort, wasted time and money, and decline of the entire company.

If people feel they have no real control over their environment and no meaningful purpose in their work, they will start to resent you, the leader, and end up leaving. Customers may become disenfranchised, too, as expectations are not fully met and they begin to question whether they are doing business with an unstable and inexperienced company.

PERSISTENCE AND CONSISTENCY ARE KEY, AND THE KEY TO CONSISTENCY IS HAVING CLEAR GOALS AND PLANS. OTHERWISE, YOUR PEOPLE AND YOUR CUSTOMERS GET CONFUSED. YOU CAN'T JUST DELIVER A MESSAGE THAT SUCH-AND-SUCH IS OUR BIG FOCUS THIS MONTH. YOU HAVE TO BEHAVE CONSISTENTLY OVER THE LONG TERM SO THAT PEOPLE KNOW HOW YOU WILL REACT TO A GIVEN SITUATION, TIME AND TIME AGAIN.

# APPLYING YOUR ENTREPRENEURIAL SKILLS

Shed old habits and create new ones based on your key entrepreneurial skills: creativity and vision. These skills can be highly instrumental in your ability to move from the Doer and Decision-Maker mode of operating to Delegator and Direction Setter. For instance, your creativity can help you develop a unique way of planning that encourages others to join you in being visionary and focused on high standards. Together with your people, develop a plan for the company's growth as well as a plan for the structures and systems, and make the plans strong and flexible enough to support future growth.

Your methods of delegating, managing, planning, and establishing structure can be nontraditional, innovative—and entrepreneurial. Your vision can inspire those to whom you are delegating parts of your job to excel in their new responsibilities. Your extensive problem-solving skills can be used to redefine your leadership role, style, and habits for the next stage of growth.

YOU HAVE TO ALWAYS BE ON THE LOOKOUT FOR SIGNS THAT IT'S TIME TO CHANGE. ONE OF MY DEFINING MOMENTS WAS WHEN WE WERE AT 25 PEOPLE. AT 7:30 IN THE MORNING, I WAS DRIVING DOWN THE HIGHWAY AT 80 MILES AN HOUR, LATE FOR AN APPOINTMENT, AND TALKING ON THE PHONE TO MY EMPLOYEES. TRAFFIC STOPPED IN FRONT OF ME AND I WAS SO WRAPPED UP IN WHAT I WAS DOING THAT I HAD TO SWERVE OFF THE ROAD TO AVOID AN ACCIDENT. I ALMOST ROLLED MY CAR. THAT'S WHEN I SAID, "I NEED TO DO THINGS DIFFERENTLY!"

I REACHED A POINT WHEN I REALIZED I WAS REALLY GOOD AT ALL THE BUSINESS STUFF—MARKETING PRESENTATIONS, TECHNICAL IMPROVEMENTS IN THE PRODUCTS, THE BUSINESS MODEL—BUT THAT TO GROW THE COMPANY, I HAD TO LEARN A WHOLE NEW SET OF THINGS ABOUT LEADERSHIP THAT I HAD NEVER LEARNED BEFORE. I BEGAN TO USE MANAGEMENT BOOKS AND GAVE THEM TO THE WHOLE TEAM. IT WAS MY PERSONAL GOAL TO LEARN HOW TO MASTER THIS WHOLE AREA OF LEADERSHIP AS WELL AS I HAD MASTERED ENGINEERING AND BUSINESS. I WAS PASSIONATE ABOUT IT, AND IT WAS FUN.

WITH THE HELP OF A CONSULTANT, WE DEFINED AND COMMUNICATED A NEW VIEW OF WHERE WE WERE HEADED AS A COMPANY WITH A SET OF VALUES FOR OUR CULTURE, AND WE SET UP A BUNCH OF TEAMS TO TAKE ON HIGH-PRIORITY TASKS IN SOME CREATIVE NEW WAYS. THE WHOLE PROCESS STIMULATED THE ENTREPRENEURIAL SPIRIT IN EVERYONE. I PRACTICED MY NEW LEADERSHIP SKILLS AND THE COMPANY CONTINUED TO GROW.

# SUMMARY:
# INITIAL GROWTH STAGE

## COMPANY GOALS

- Launch a product that offers something different.
- Grow revenues.
- Capture market share.

## COMPANY CHARACTERISTICS

- Fast-paced
- Highly flexible/willing to experiment
- Often chaotic
- Sales-driven
- Close to customers
- Feels like a "real" company for the first time

## RED FLAGS: SIGNALS FOR CHANGING YOUR ROLE

- Days are too short.
- Physically/emotionally impossible to do everything you need to do.
- People want your time but can't seem to get it.
- Everyone is constantly fighting fires.
- You don't know which of multiple growth opportunities to pursue.
- You feel pressure because you're managing all the risks alone.

*cont...*

-CONTINUED

## DANGERS IF YOU DON'T CHANGE

- You will be resented as a micromanager and a bottleneck.

- People will be demotivated and wait for you to make all decisions.

- Priorities will constantly change as a "strategy-du-jour" or "ideas-of-the-moment" management style dominates.

- The company will lose focus.

- Growth will be impeded; the company will decline.

## KEY LEADERSHIP ROLES

- Delegator

- Direction Setter

## CRITICAL RESPONSIBILITIES

- Articulate and communicate your vision and values.

- Understand your personal goals for the long term.

- Use scarce resources creatively.

- Watch critical performance indicators, especially financial ones.

- Integrate input from stakeholders with your own perspective.

- Hire multitalented people whose values match yours.

- Use mentors.

## PERSONAL CHANGES TO MAKE IN YOUR LEADERSHIP ROLE

- Focus, focus, focus.

- Manage proactively, not reactively.

- Begin delegating your responsibilities; establish systems and a structure with clearly defined roles, responsibilities, and priorities.

- Stop making all the decisions.

- Stop solving all the problems and answering all questions.

- Trust others; make them accountable for results.

- Start planning for the future instead of shooting from the hip and reacting to every new opportunity.

- Accept the need for processes and structure.

- Share credit and limelight with others.

- Consciously spend a portion of your time working on the big picture of your business, not just the day-to-day operations.

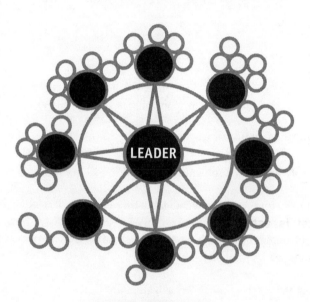

**RAPID GROWTH**

**Team Builder
Coach
Planner
Communicator**

# CHAPTER 3

# RAPID GROWTH

When we were 20 people and I was in my hands-on mode, everyone understood our risks and challenges and was on the same page. Now that we're at 70 and moving as fast as we can to recruit more people, the challenges are much more complex. There are expectations to meet from all angles: the board, the management team, employees and customers. Our market is established now; the competition is fiercer, the stakes are bigger, and all the lights are on the company and on me—and every move I make.

THERE ARE THREE ELEMENTS IN THE DYNAMIC RIGHT NOW: THE PRODUCT IS READY AND PROVEN, THE MARKET IS GROWING LIKE MAD, AND THE ORGANIZATION NEEDS TO MATURE. THE PRESSURE IS HUGE SINCE A WINNER IN THE MARKET WILL BE DECLARED SOON, AND WE HAVE TO FIGURE OUT HOW TO LEVERAGE OUR ADVANTAGES AND MANAGE OUR DISADVANTAGES. AT THIS CRITICAL TIME, I'M WORRIED THAT I'M NOT MAKING THE STRATEGIC IMPACT I SHOULD BE MAKING AS THE CEO, BECAUSE THE THINGS THAT ONLY I CAN DO TO GET THE SMALLEST PORTION OF MY TIME. FOR EXAMPLE, I'M SPENDING THE BIGGEST PERCENTAGE OF MY TIME ON THE FINANCIAL PIECE VERSUS GETTING OTHER PEOPLE TO THINK DIFFERENTLY ABOUT GROWING THE BUSINESS. IT IS VERY IMPORTANT THAT I PLAY THE RIGHT ROLE AS LEADER NOW BECAUSE I'VE LEARNED THAT WHAT YOU DO TO GET YOUR FIRST POSITION IN THE MARKET IS DIFFERENT FROM WHAT YOU MUST DO TO PREPARE ALL THE TROOPS TO ACTUALLY COMPETE HEAD-ON AND WIN A SIGNIFICANT SHARE OF THE MARKET.

# YOUR COMPANY'S NEW GOALS IN RAPID GROWTH

In Chapter 2 you learned that successfully navigating the Initial Growth stage requires that you develop a strategy, a structure, and adopt a more proactive leadership style. These changes provide the strength, depth, and stability needed to support your company's faster rate of growth during Initial Growth. However, as the company enters the second stage of growth, Rapid Growth, the focus changes. In this stage, you need to develop and communicate a new set of goals that will help the company achieve widespread use of its products and services, gain significant market share, ward off competitors, and move into a market leadership position.

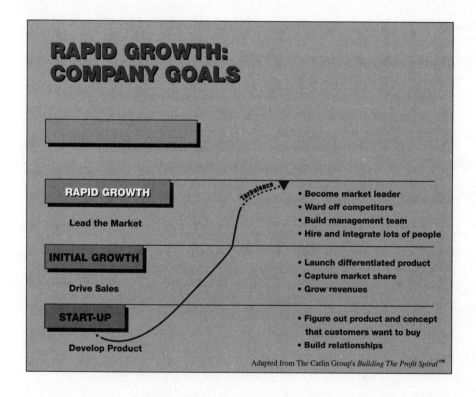

**RAPID GROWTH: COMPANY GOALS**

**RAPID GROWTH**

Lead the Market

- Become market leader
- Ward off competitors
- Build management team
- Hire and integrate lots of people

**INITIAL GROWTH**

Drive Sales

- Launch differentiated product
- Capture market share
- Grow revenues

**START-UP**

Develop Product

- Figure out product and concept that customers want to buy
- Build relationships

Adapted from The Catlin Group's *Building The Profit Spiral*™

You must continually strengthen your company's infrastructure and develop effective processes and systems to support this aggressive growth. You will need to add new people with expertise in different functional areas, for example, finance, marketing, organization development. Then you will need to build a strong management team, one that will plan the development of the company's growth and determine what metrics to use and how to measure progress against plan. Hiring, integrating, and managing more people with outstanding talent are clear priorities. And, perhaps most crucial, you will need to align all the groups that have a stake in the company's success—employees, customers, prospects, and investors—and keep them in alignment (see the preceding figure).

## RED FLAGS: WARNING SIGNS THAT TELL YOU IT'S TIME TO CHANGE ROLES

Moving into Rapid Growth feels like moving from a swiftly moving stream into whitewater rapids: It's exhilarating, but very scary. The pace is so fast that your adrenaline seems to be flowing constantly. This period feels drastically different from Initial Growth, when you had more time to consider the pros and cons of decisions and to learn new things. Now, you feel like you're betting the company's future every day without adequate time or information for decision making. At the same time, you have to do everything *exactly* right or it will all blow up.

Here are some signals that your company is moving into the Rapid Growth stage and that your leadership role needs to change once again:

 The pressures are mounting, and it's beginning to be way too hard to get things done. You feel like you're always behind the curve and find yourself wishing for more and faster systems for all kinds of processes: information management, lead qualification, sales-pipeline management, product development and launch, quality control, shipping and delivery, inventory control, and hiring/training new people.

 You realize that product and market development must expand because customers are demanding more from you.

*cont...*

*-continued*

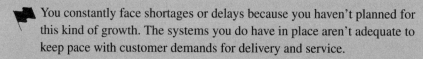 You constantly face shortages or delays because you haven't planned for this kind of growth. The systems you do have in place aren't adequate to keep pace with customer demands for delivery and service.

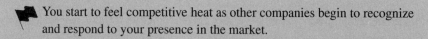 You start to feel competitive heat as other companies begin to recognize and respond to your presence in the market.

You have to hire a lot of people quickly, but finding the talent when you need it is very tough.

You find yourself longing for true experts because there are big gaps in the company's areas of functional expertise.

Some of your original employees are growing and taking on bigger responsibilities, but others look like they're not going to make it—and it's painful to think about what that means for their future at the company.

You want to mold your management team into a well-oiled machine, with each person fully understanding the part he or she must play, but you're not sure how to do it. You worry that your managers are not proactive enough; that they have their heads down, focusing only on operational issues; and that they aren't keeping their eyes on the big picture and planning ahead.

There is so much going on internally, you worry that people are losing touch with what's happening in the external environment.

With all the growth you're experiencing, you haven't yet figured out the best kind of financing for continued growth.

The original culture is changing dramatically. The small-family feeling has disappeared, and people miss it. You don't even know everyone's name any more.

It's hard to imagine the pace getting any faster, but it seems to go up a notch every day.

I WAS BURNING OUT. THERE WE WERE, GROWING LIKE MAD, AND I HAD NO ENERGY OR EXCITEMENT ABOUT IT. I STARTED WORKING WITH A COACH AND EVENTUALLY REALIZED I WAS THE PROBLEM. I WAS MICROMANAGING. SO I DEVELOPED A PERSONAL VISION AND THEN A COMPANY VISION, AND ASKED MY MANAGEMENT TEAM TO GO THROUGH THE SAME EXERCISE. I TOLD THEM I WANTED TO RESIGN AS THEIR BOSS, AND I HOPED THEY WOULD INVITE ME TO BE THEIR COACH. TOGETHER, WE TIGHTENED UP ROLE DESCRIPTIONS, PROCESSES, AND POLICIES. WE BROUGHT IN SOME NEW PEOPLE AND SOME PEOPLE LEFT. I LEARNED THAT I WAS A TERRIBLE LISTENER AND WAS STIFLING IDEAS AND INSIGHTS OF OTHERS BY MAKING MY OWN STATEMENT AFTER EACH PERSON MADE THEIRS. NOW I LET EVERYONE TALK AND I LISTEN. MY MANAGEMENT TEAM CAME UP WITH A GREAT NEW MISSION AND STATEMENT OF PURPOSE AND VALUES FOR THE COMPANY THAT WERE BETTER THAN ANYTHING I COULD HAVE PUT TOGETHER. MY BIG LESSON WAS THAT IF I WANTED TO TAKE THIS COMPANY FORWARD, I HAD TO ADMIT MY FAULTS AND TRY TO CHANGE. I GUESS I DID A PRETTY MAJOR MAKEOVER. AND IT'S GREAT. THE COMPANY IS DOING BETTER THAN EVER—AND I'M EXCITED AGAIN.

I'LL NEVER FORGET THE FIRST TIME I WALKED INTO THE LAB AND DISCUSSION STOPPED. I THOUGHT I'D DIE. WE HAD BEEN SUCH A CLOSE GROUP, BUT WITH THE ADVENT OF MORE AND MORE EMPLOYEES AND WORK I REALIZED NOW I WAS "THE BOSS." I GRIEVED THE LOSS BUT ADJUSTED.

# YOUR ROLES AND KEY RESPONSIBILITIES

During Initial Growth, you had two primary, overarching roles: Delegator and Direction Setter. In Rapid Growth, you must dramatically change those roles and take on four new ones. This is why the circle in the following illustration that signifies your role in Rapid Growth is smaller than before, and the circles that signify your top management team are equal in size to yours. You no longer make all the decisions; your team has an equal role in decision making. Your new role is

- Team Builder
- Coach

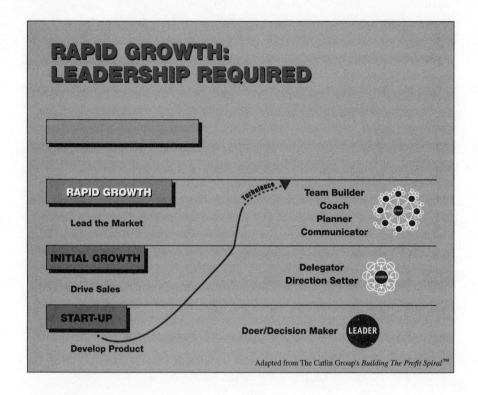

**RAPID GROWTH: LEADERSHIP REQUIRED**

RAPID GROWTH — Turbulence — Team Builder / Coach / Planner / Communicator

Lead the Market

INITIAL GROWTH — Delegator / Direction Setter

Drive Sales

START-UP — Doer/Decision Maker — LEADER

Develop Product

Adapted from The Catlin Group's *Building The Profit Spiral*™

- Planner
- Communicator

It's important to move into these four new roles as soon as possible. You need to focus your time and energy on building your management team, building a shared plan, and building a strong infrastructure for Rapid Growth. Many entrepreneurs we've interviewed lamented the fact that they didn't make these changes earlier.

The lesson here is to be more proactive in recognizing what the company needs, and to do so before you hit a wall and have to make the needed changes while in crisis mode. You must anticipate the required changes and start early to make the transitions needed to move the company successfully into the Rapid Growth stage.

> WHEN WE STARTED REALLY BUILDING SOME DEPTH INTO OUR MANAGEMENT TEAM, THE COMPANY WAS SOMEWHERE BETWEEN $15 MILLION AND $17 MILLION. THE ISSUE FOR US WAS NOT HOW TO GET FROM $15 MILLION TO $22 MILLION. THE ISSUE WAS HOW TO GET FROM $15 MILLION TO $100 MILLION.

To do that, we had to have a focus and a strategy, and so on: a real plan that gave people powerful roles in forming strategy and making decisions. It meant I had to let go of some of what I had always done. But once we did it, it freed us to grow like crazy. People want—they need—to have a clear direction and a clear strategy and a clear set of objectives. And then they can really fly.

## Team Builder

In your role as Team Builder, you must hire and/or develop a management team of functional experts that is strong enough to keep the company together and develop its full potential for successful growth. The first step is to be ruthlessly honest in determining your own personal strengths and weaknesses as well as those of your original team. Get feedback from people you trust. This process can help you see yourself more clearly so that you can redefine your own role to capitalize on your personal strengths. Then you can hire others to complement your weaknesses and can direct your efforts in ways that will have the biggest payoff.

A good leader has to be conscious of his or her limitations and has to have plans for getting past those limitations. If he (or she) can't, he has to make some hard decisions for the benefit of the company. You have to recognize what you need to do differently and adapt to it.

You can't lead every aspect of the business any more—you just don't have the expertise in every single area of the business as it scales. Identify the weaknesses in your team, including your own, and go hire the best in the world to bring experience and super skills to the company. Find people you can trust and really learn from. Be aggressive in getting the people you really want. Then learn to get just far enough out of their way so that they surprise you with smart decisions.

Make a list of your strengths and weaknesses and of the strengths and weaknesses of everyone else in your organization. Then look at the functional work that needs to be done in such areas as sales, marketing, finance, product development, and organizational development. Define the gaps where you need additional expertise and experience. Designate each skill set as a long- or short-term need. When you hire, look for people to fit the long-term needs of the company. Fill in the gaps to create a truly balanced, complementary team with diverse skills. You want people who are smarter than you are in the functional areas of expertise but who share your values and exhibit your entrepreneurial strengths.

RESIST THE TEMPTATION TO HIRE PEOPLE YOU CAN CONTROL AND WHO WILL ALWAYS FOLLOW YOUR PATTERN. HIRE PEOPLE WHO ARE SMARTER THAN YOU.

I WAS GIVEN BAD ADVICE IN THE EARLY STAGES OF THE COMPANY. I WAS TOLD NOT TO HIRE PEOPLE WHO WERE MORE EXPENSIVE OR MORE EXPERIENCED THAN WE NEEDED AT THE TIME. SO WE GOT PEOPLE WHOSE JOBS HAVE NOW OUTGROWN THEM IN ONLY 18 MONTHS. IT WOULD HAVE BEEN BETTER TO BRING IN A SENIOR-LEVEL PERSON A YEAR AGO AT A VP LEVEL THAN HAVE SOMEONE WHO CAN'T KEEP UP AND NOW WE HAVE TO BRING IN A VP ANYWAY.

HIRING SMART PEOPLE IS A DIFFICULT THING FOR AN ENTREPRENEUR WITH LITTLE OR NO TRAINING IN THE SUBJECT. FOR EXAMPLE, EARLY IN MY CAREER I THOUGHT ANYBODY WITH AN MBA FROM A PRESTIGIOUS SCHOOL HAD TO BE SMARTER THAN I WAS. HAVING WORKED WITH A LOT OF THEM, WHAT I'VE LEARNED IS THAT THEY WERE ONLY BETTER EDUCATED THAN I WAS BUT NOT NECESSARILY SMARTER. LEARNING HOW TO IDENTIFY SMART PEOPLE AND KNOWING WHEN YOU HAVE THE RIGHT ONE IS CRITICAL.

To assemble your entrepreneurial team, look for achievement-oriented, self-motivated managers with the ambition to build something significant. They must also demonstrate the values you believe are important and that fit with the entrepreneurial culture you want to create.

THE PEOPLE YOU HIRE HAVE TO HAVE THE RAW MATERIAL TO BEGIN WITH, QUALITIES LIKE INTELLIGENCE, MOTIVATION, AND THE DESIRE TO SUCCEED. THEY HAVE TO SHARE THE COMPANY'S VALUES. AND THEY HAVE TO KNOW HOW TO MAKE MISTAKES, RECOGNIZE WHEN THEY HAVE MADE MISTAKES, ADMIT THAT, AND CORRECT THEM. THOSE ARE THE PEOPLE YOU NEED.

THERE NEEDS TO BE A LOT OF LEADERS IN ONE ORGANIZATION. ONE THING A LEADER DOES IS CREATE OTHER LEADERS. THAT'S THE ONLY WAY TO BE SURE YOU CAN DELEGATE RESPONSIBILITIES TO SOMEONE YOU TRUST.

Finally, after assembling the top team with the expertise you need, your goal is to make sure your group of managers works as a true team. You must be the team leader who helps all members of the team learn to work together productively, with trust and respect. They need to develop the skills to communicate, resolve disagreements, solve company issues openly and creatively, and truly leverage each other's strengths and skills. This is easier said than done, and in the beginning it's a lot like herding cats. But effective teamwork that fully capitalizes on the members' complementary strengths is critical in leading the company's growth. Your entrepreneurial team must be on the same page and act as a role model for all other teams in the company. The company cannot and will not grow if the top team is not focused and cohesive, and not good decision makers.

AFTER STARTING AND BUILDING TWO COMPANIES, I'VE LEARNED A FEW THINGS ABOUT MANAGING GROWTH. IF YOU WANT TO TAKE OFF LIKE A ROCKET, GETTING THE FUNDING FOR GROWTH IS THE ROCKET FUEL. BUT THE *ONLY* WAY TO GROW IS TO BRING IN A FULL TEAM OF REALLY STRONG VPS WHO CAN BE THE ROCKET ENGINES. THEN YOUR RESPONSIBILITY IS TO LEARN HOW TO MANAGE THEM. THEY NEED TO BE HARNESSED AND DIRECTED SO THEY *WORK TOGETHER.* THE HARD PART IS THAT THEY'RE HIGHLY EGOTISTICAL AND INDEPENDENT (THAT'S WHY YOU HIRED THEM), SO THEY'LL TELL YOU THEY DON'T NEED TO BE HARNESSED AND DIRECTED. BUT IF YOU DON'T GIVE THAT DIRECTION, THEY'LL COMPETE WITH EACH OTHER AND BUILD THEIR OWN POWER STRUCTURES AS SEPARATE ENTITIES WITHIN THE COMPANY. THAT'S THE *LAST* THING YOU NEED FOR FAST GROWTH. THE ROCKET ENGINES MUST MOVE THE ROCKET IN THE SAME DIRECTION OR THE WHOLE THING WILL EXPLODE.

PART OF SETTING THE DIRECTION FOR THE TEAM IS SAYING NO TO THESE PEOPLE IF THEY'RE GOING OFF THE STRATEGY. YOU MUST CONSTANTLY BE FOCUSED ON THE BIG PICTURE AND REMINDING PEOPLE OF THE DIRECTION, EVALUATING OPTIONS AGAINST THAT DIRECTION AND THEN SAYING YES OR NO. THEN EVERYONE WILL LEARN HOW TO MAKE THEIR OWN YES/NO DECISIONS WITH THE RIGHT CRITERIA.

THAT'S LEADERSHIP—AND IT'S HARD. IF YOU CAN DO IT, YOU'LL BE STRAPPED TO THE ROCKET. IF YOU CAN'T DO THAT WITH THE TEAM, GET SOMEONE ELSE WHO CAN. THAT'S WHAT I HAD TO DO IN MY FIRST COMPANY, AND IT HAS SINCE GROWN LIKE WILDFIRE.

## COACH

As Coach, you delegate responsibility, provide guidance, and help each team member succeed by doing four things:

**1.** Clearly define each individual's role and areas of accountability.

**2.** Set goals together that foster cooperation and synergy.

**3.** Assign responsibility and authority to make specific types of decisions.

**4.** Delineate parameters for other decisions that require your input and/or the input of other team members.

Once you've accomplished those four tasks, you have to allow these individuals to use their strengths and do their jobs. Give frequent feedback, teach them what you know, stretch them, and encourage them to feel pride in their accomplishments. Hold them accountable—with clear measures of success—for achieving results, for using their expertise, and for coaching and developing their own people.

YOU HAVE TO GET INTO THE POSITION TO SAY TO ALL YOUR TEAM MEMBERS, "YOU'RE RUNNING THIS THING, AND I'M STANDING BEHIND YOU. BUT THIS IS WHAT I'M SEEING, AND MAYBE SOME FEEDBACK WILL BE HELPFUL." YOU NEED TO LEARN HOW TO CRITIQUE WHAT THEY *DO* WITHOUT CRITICIZING *THEM*. GET THEM TO START SHIFTING INTO STRATEGIC THINKING AND PLANNING, BECAUSE UNTIL THEY PARTICIPATE IN THE STRATEGIC VISIONING OF THE COMPANY, THEY WILL NEVER BE FULLY PERCEIVED AS LEADERS IN THEIR OWN RIGHT. IT WILL ALWAYS SEEM LIKE THE LEADERSHIP IS COMING FROM SOMEWHERE ELSE, AND THEY'RE JUST EXECUTIONERS OR MANAGERS.

EMPOWERMENT IS THE KEY TO LEADERSHIP. I TELL MY PEOPLE THAT IF THEY MAKE A DECISION THAT'S GOOD FOR THE COMPANY AND GOOD FOR THE CUSTOMER, IT'S THE RIGHT DECISION. WE'LL DISCUSS THE DETAILS LATER; AND IF THE DECISION WASN'T TOTALLY CORRECT, WE'LL LEARN FROM IT. BUT MAKE THE DECISION, BE SELF-SUFFICIENT, AND BE PART OF THE TEAM.

# Planner

As Planner, you lead the team in creating a strategic roadmap for growth, with a shared vision and mission for the company and with proactive strategies for the following:

- Capitalizing on market opportunities
- Ensuring positioning and brand awareness that gives your company competitive advantages
- Managing sales, distribution, and internal operations
- Fostering continual innovation in products and services
- Hiring, training, and managing an awesome work force

You need to guide a participative process that addresses key questions about your company: Who are we? Why are we better than anyone else? What's our "unfair" competitive advantage? Where is the best opportunity for market leadership? and What are the ways to keep on top of the market?

THE SINGLE BIGGEST THING IN ENABLING OUR FAST GROWTH WAS GETTING PEOPLE TO UNDERSTAND WHAT OUR ADVANTAGE REALLY WAS, AND WHY IT WAS A SUSTAINABLE ADVANTAGE. THE NEXT WAS BUILDING A SET OF STRATEGIC OBJECTIVES THAT PEOPLE COULD SEE WE COULD WIN AT, AND WIN AT CONSISTENTLY. AND THEN HAVING A CLEAR POSITIONING.

SALES-DRIVEN STRATEGIES ARE IMPORTANT AT EARLIER STAGES OF A COMPANY'S LIFE, BUT IF YOU'RE TOTALLY SALES DRIVEN YOU END UP REACTING TO EVERY OPPORTUNITY. YOU SCURRY OVER AND GET THIS SALE, AND YOU SCURRY OVER AND GET THAT ONE; AND YOU DON'T REALLY HAVE A FOCUS, A DIRECTION, OR A SUSTAINABLE STRATEGIC POSITION. THE SINGLE THING THAT WE CREATED WAS AN UNDERSTANDING OF WHO WE ARE, WHAT OUR ADVANTAGE IS, AREAS WHERE WE'RE BETTER THAN EVERYBODY ELSE, AND HOW BIG WE THINK THIS OPPORTUNITY IS IF WE ALIGN ALL OF OUR ENERGY IN THIS DIRECTION. I THINK THAT GETTING PEOPLE TO UNDERSTAND THAT THERE WAS A SPACE THAT WAS MEANINGFUL, AND SPACE IN WHICH WE COULD WIN, WAS THE SINGLE MOST IMPORTANT THING WE DID WHICH LED TO OUR SUCCESS.

TO ACHIEVE GROWTH AND CHANGE, YOU MUST FIRST HAVE A CLEAR VISION AND THEN A GAME PLAN TO TAKE YOU THERE. IF YOU'RE TRYING TO FIGURE OUT WHAT YOUR BUSINESS IS ABOUT, YOU'VE GOT TO GET THAT DONE QUICKLY.

USE OUTSIDERS, IF NECESSARY; THEY CAN BE VERY HELPFUL. BUT YOU'VE GOT TO GET THAT DONE QUICKLY, BECAUSE THE ORGANIZATION IS WAITING FOR THE VISION AND THE PLAN.

YOU CAN'T DEFINE A GAME PLAN UNLESS YOU KNOW WHERE YOU'RE GOING. WHEN I GET IN MY AIRPLANE, I KNOW WHERE I'M GOING. THE GAME PLAN IS JUST HOW I GET THERE. THERE HAVE BEEN TIMES WHEN I'VE BEEN IN THE CLOUDS, WHEN I HAVEN'T KNOWN WHERE I WAS GOING, AND IT WAS VERY UNCOMFORTABLE—AND DANGEROUS FOR ME AND MY PLANE.

Capture in writing the answers to those key questions. Then develop and communicate a plan that represents the team's agreement on priorities and actions to achieve the mission, vision, and strategies over the next 12 to 24 months; and specify clear goals, action steps, financial performance expectations, and metrics for measuring milestones and evaluating success. The plan should include changes needed in the organizational structure; processes for effective management and reporting of progress; plans and programs for attracting, retaining, and developing people; and a system for recognizing and rewarding results.

In addition, the plan must contain a section that defines the culture and values, an area that's often overlooked in company plans. Attention to culture and values will foster accountability, teamwork, creative ideas, proactive problem solving, and effective communication—all in support of the company vision for growth.

One planning process, called Building the Profit Spiral™, was developed by The Catlin Group especially for entrepreneurs and has enabled many companies to develop the plans, teams, and skills needed for growth. This process enables organizations committed to healthy growth to move smoothly through the stages of growth by looping five critical elements—Market and Customer Focus, Mission and Values, Vision and Objectives, Strategies and Plans, and Structure and Processes—around a sixth element, Innovative Culture, which acts as the supporting core (see the following figure).

The development of The Profit Spiral™, as well as the process of defining each element for your company, is vital to continuing growth and success.

You and your leadership team must gain consensus on the definition and development of these loops, so that each provides the foundation for the next one, and all are perfectly aligned. You must then involve the rest of your organization by establishing teams, systems, processes, and learning opportunities that empower people to successfully implement the strategies needed to move toward the vision. All this must be done collaboratively in an environment conducive to performance, innovation, and growth.

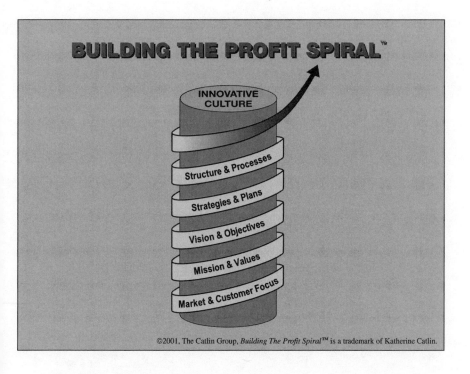

©2001, The Catlin Group, *Building The Profit Spiral*™ is a trademark of Katherine Catlin.

WE STARTED OUR NEW PLANNING PROCESS BY EVALUATING OUR BUSINESS. WE TOOK 15 SENIOR PEOPLE THROUGH EXTENSIVE INTERVIEWS. PEOPLE REALLY OPENED UP, AND WE GOT ALL THE GOOD NEWS, THE BAD NEWS, AND THE UGLY TRUTHS OUT ON THE TABLE. THAT'S WHAT YOU REALLY NEED TO DO. ALL OF THIS HELPED US CLARIFY WHAT TARGET MARKETS WE WANTED TO GO AFTER. IT HELPED US SEE THAT WE WERE SPREAD TOO THIN TRYING TO SERVE TOO MANY MARKETS. WE NEEDED TO NARROW OUR FOCUS. I DISCOVERED MY VIEW OF THE FUTURE DIFFERED FROM OTHER PEOPLE'S IDEAS. THEY HAD VERY DIFFERENT PICTURES OF THE COMPANY—SIZE, ATTRIBUTES, VALUE PROPOSITION—WHICH MEANT THEY HAD DIFFERENT VIEWS ON STRATEGY, TOO. WE TALKED A LOT ABOUT THAT IN OFF-SITE MEETINGS, EXPLORING WHAT THE SIMILARITIES WERE IN OUR VISIONS AND WHAT THE REAL DIFFERENCES WERE. A CONSENSUS EMERGED. AND THE VISION WE ENDED UP WITH WAS BETTER THAN MY ORIGINAL ONE. IT WAS MORE SPECIFIC AND CONCRETE. IT HAD NEW IDEAS I HADN'T CONSIDERED. BUT MORE IMPORTANT, IT WASN'T MY IDEA. IT CAME FROM 15 TOP MANAGERS, AND THEY REALLY FELT IT WAS THEIR WORK, NOT MINE.

THE PROCESS ALSO HELPED ME CRYSTALIZE MY THINKING ABOUT WHAT I WANTED TO DO ABOUT ORGANIZATIONAL CHANGES, HOW FAST I WANTED TO DO IT, AND WHO I WANTED TO PUT IN WHICH POSITIONS. IT BECAME CLEAR TO ME THAT A GREAT SENSE OF URGENCY AND EXCITEMENT WAS WELLING UP AS

# VITAL SIGNS: ELEMENTS OF BUILDING THE PROFIT SPIRAL™

**Market and Customer Focus**—company-wide knowledge of highest potential markets and customer groups.

*What do our customers and target prospects value most? Why? Why will they want to buy from us? How are we constantly staying in close touch with them?*

**Mission and Values**—a powerful and compelling sense of purpose and beliefs.

*Who are we in business to serve? What do we enable our customers to do so they can win? What distinguishes us from everyone else? What do we stand for? What do our customers and our target prospects value most? Why? Why will they want to buy from us? How are we constantly staying in close touch with them?*

**Vision and Objectives**—a specific picture of the ideal future.

*Where are we going? What will be new, different, and better two to three years from now in all aspects of the business: products/services, market position, core competencies, operations, marketing and sales, infrastructure, people and teams, and financial growth?*

**Strategies and Plans**—goals, action plans, and milestones that achieve the vision and that satisfy customers, differentiate us from competition, and manage internal strengths and weaknesses.

*How are we getting there? What are the annual and quarterly roadmaps for the overall company and for each functional department? What are the critical milestones and metrics?*

**Structure and Processes**—clearly defined roles, responsibilities, and accountabilities.

*How are we managing the plan? How does the work flow efficiently? Who's doing what? How are people linked? How are they rewarded?*

**Innovative Culture**—an environment empowering people to perform at their best.

*Under what fundamental principles and values do we operate? How are we promoting and supporting customer focus, communication, collaboration, creativity, constructive leadership, continuous learning, and the management of change?*

PART OF THIS PROCESS. SOME COMPANIES WAIT TOO LONG TO MAKE THE ORGANIZATIONAL CHANGES THAT WILL DRIVE THE EXCITING NEW STRATEGY. THEY END UP DISSIPATING A LOT OF THE MOMENTUM.

WE ELIMINATED BUSINESS UNITS AND CREATED CROSS-FUNCTIONAL TEAMS OF PRODUCT DEVELOPMENT, SALES, SUPPORT, AND MARKETING. ONE OF THE IMPORTANT UNDERSTANDINGS THAT CAME OUT OF THE PLANNING WORK WAS THAT WE WERE DOING MARKETING PROGRAMS INSTEAD OF STRATEGIC MARKETING. WE NEEDED A MUCH MORE STRATEGIC UNDERSTANDING OF CUSTOMER NEEDS AND MARKET CONDITIONS TO FULFILL OUR MISSION, SOMETHING MANY COMPANIES HAVE A HARD TIME DOING. WE'RE QUITE EXCITED ABOUT GETTING CLOSER TO CUSTOMERS. WE'RE DOING MUCH CLOSER ANALYSIS OF CUSTOMER MARKETS AND THEIR PATTERNS.

WE USED A CONSULTANT TO HELP WITH THIS WHOLE PROCESS, BUT WE MADE OUR OWN DISCOVERIES AND DECISIONS. IN THE END, WE CREATED THREE IMPORTANT THINGS: A MUCH MORE FOCUSED STRATEGY FOR GROWTH, A MUCH MORE COMMITTED AND UNIFIED TEAM, AND A SET OF PROCESSES ABOUT HOW TO DO IT, OVER AND OVER AGAIN, AS THE MARKET CONSTANTLY CHANGES AND WE KEEP ADAPTING.

A plan defines the focal points of mission, vision, values, and market-driven strategy. It also creates a guide for the development of functional plans, individual job-performance standards, and measurement systems that tie directly to the compensation systems. Once the plan is defined, you still need an ongoing process to help the team manage the plan, measure results with key metrics, adjust the plan to market shifts, communicate progress, and refocus everyone in the company, as necessary. This requires weekly, monthly, quarterly, and annual meetings. Yes, meetings! Entrepreneurs who avoid meetings are entrepreneurs who have not yet learned how effective regular, *productive* meetings can be.

> YOU HAVE TO CREATE AN ENVIRONMENT WHERE LEADERS CAN EMERGE. SOMETIMES THAT MEANS GIVING UP SOME OF THE WAYS YOU MANAGE, WHICH INCLUDES AVOIDING MEETINGS. EVERYONE SAYS THEY HATE MEETINGS. BUT WE'VE LEARNED THE IMPORTANCE OF REGULAR MEETINGS, TO STAY FOCUSED AND INFORMED.

Finally, as Planner, you and the team members must engage in well-organized discussions to compare your observations of the outside world and to review feedback from others about your company. It's the only way to pick up signs of change in the competitive picture and to make sure your company is reflecting those changes in the marketplace. Be an outspoken champion for market and customer information because it's easy for that to slip through the cracks as the fast pace of growth continues. During Rapid Growth, there's a danger that everyone will be so internally focused on growing the company that they will lose sight of the market and miss changes that will hugely impact the company. Make sure that people have multiple sources for accessing this information about markets and customers; then take time to discuss it. These regular discussions will enable you and the team to track and incorporate new opportunities that fit the vision and plan for growth.

> YOU NEED REAL-WORLD FEEDBACK. AND AS A CEO YOUR JOB IS HOLDING UP THE MIRROR TO THE ORGANIZATION AND SAYING, "HEY, THIS IS WHAT WE REALLY LOOK LIKE." MAYBE YOU HAVE TO DO IT WITH HELP FROM CUSTOMERS. MAYBE YOU HAVE TO DO IT WITH HELP FROM INDUSTRY ANALYSTS. MAYBE YOU HAVE TO DO IT WITH HELP FROM YOUR INVESTORS, IF YOU HAVE OUTSIDE INVESTORS. AND SOMETIMES YOU HAVE TO BE A LITTLE BIT BRUTAL, I THINK, BECAUSE IF YOU'RE KIDDING YOURSELF, OR "DRINKING YOUR OWN BATH WATER," AS WE SAY, THAT'S A SERIOUS PROBLEM.

## COMMUNICATOR

> COMMUNICATION IS INCREDIBLY IMPORTANT. IT'S IMPOSSIBLE TO OVER-COMMUNICATE WITH YOUR EXECUTIVE TEAM OR THE REST OF THE STAFF. THERE'S NO WAY TO DO IT.

As Communicator, you must take responsibility for constantly reinforcing the vision and plan by giving consistent messages. As the number of employees in the organization increases, your communication of this information helps to gain alignment and buy-in from all employees, both old and new.

ONCE WE HAD SET IN PLACE A NEW VISION AND OUR NEW GAME PLAN, WE HAD TO COMMUNICATE HOW WE WERE DOING AGAINST IT. WE, THE MANAGEMENT TEAM, WOULD MAKE A PRESENTATION TO THE COMPANY ON A QUARTERLY BASIS. SO WE SENT THE VPS TO DIFFERENT ORGANIZATIONS EACH QUARTER. THAT MEANT THE DEVELOPMENT TEAM ONE QUARTER WOULD HEAR FROM THE SALES VP, ANOTHER QUARTER WOULD HEAR FROM THE MARKETING VP, SOMEBODY OTHER THAN THEIR OWN VP. IT WAS A CHANCE FOR A LOT MORE INTERACTION, BUT EACH VP GAVE THE SAME PRESENTATION. WE PUT TOGETHER A SET OF OVERHEADS AND A POWERPOINT PRESENTATION SO PEOPLE WOULD DELIVER THE SAME MESSAGE. IT WAS A GREAT OPPORTUNITY FOR A LOT MORE INTERACTION THAN OTHERWISE WOULD HAVE TAKEN PLACE.

In addition, you must consider and coordinate the views of all constituencies, including employees, customers, partners, investors, and board members. Make sure they are constantly informed about the plan, goals, and expectations. Give them a chance to provide you with input and feedback. Calibrate your strategies and results regularly with your board of directors, and be sure to involve them heavily in strategic plans and decisions.

One way to gain alignment within the company is to provide people with data and information about markets, customers, and industry benchmarks that are directly related to the company's plan. Many companies are using "open book" management, or at least sharing information on planned-versus-actual financial performance, so employees can understand expectations, make good decisions, and take effective action.

ANOTHER CEO ONCE SAID TO ME, "VISION IS LIKE ORANGE JUICE. IT'S GOOD FOR YOU AND YOU NEED TO DRINK IT EVERY DAY." YOU TRY TO COMMUNICATE THE VISION AND THE PLAN TO PEOPLE EVERY DAY, IN COUNTLESS SMALL WAYS, AND USE THE VISION AND PLAN TO SET THE CONTEXT OF EVERY MEETING. WE ALSO HAVE ANNUAL MEETINGS WITH EVERYONE TO SHOW THEM WHERE WE HAVE BEEN, WHERE WE ARE GOING, AND HOW WE PLAN TO GET THERE. IN BETWEEN, WE CONSTANTLY REFINE AND REFRESH THAT DIRECTION—IN OTHER WORDS, WE SERVE LOTS OF ORANGE JUICE ALONG THE WAY!

WE HAVE AN ORIENTATION PROGRAM ON A MONTHLY AND A QUARTERLY BASIS, AND ONE OF THE THINGS I DO IS GO THROUGH SOME REAL BASIC STUFF

WITH THE NEW PEOPLE. I GET UP THERE WITH THE FLIP CHART AND SAY, "WHAT'S A CORPORATION? WHAT'S THE PURPOSE OF A CORPORATION?" AND I FIND ALMOST NOBODY KNOWS THE ANSWERS TO THOSE QUESTIONS. THESE QUESTIONS ARE REALLY BASIC. YOU ASK PEOPLE, AND THE FIRST THING THAT COMES OUT USUALLY IS 'MAKE PROFITS.' OR IT'S 'SERVE THE CUSTOMER,' AND YOU USUALLY GET THIS DISJOINTED LIST THAT MAKES YOU REALIZE THAT PEOPLE COME INTO WORK EVERY DAY AND DON'T KNOW WHAT THE PURPOSE OF AN ORGANIZATION REALLY IS.

I TAKE THEM THROUGH THIS EXERCISE BECAUSE I THINK IT'S IMPORTANT FOR THEM TO UNDERSTAND THE DEFINITION: "A CORPORATION IS SIMPLY AN ORGANIZATION THAT SERVES A CONSTITUENCY." AND THEN I HAVE THEM BRAIN-STORM WHAT THE CONSTITUENCY IS OF AN ORGANIZATION, AND THEN WE COME UP WITH SIX: EMPLOYEES, STOCKHOLDERS, CUSTOMERS, VENDORS, PARTNERS, AND COMMUNITY.

ONCE YOU HAVE THAT LIST YOU CAN SAY, "WELL, WHAT DOES IT MEAN FOR A COMPANY TO BE SUCCESSFUL? HOW DO YOU DEFINE SUCCESS?" AND SUCCESS IS SIMPLY MEASURED AS SERVING YOUR CONSTITUENCIES WELL. IT'S NOT PROFITS. IT'S NOT MAKING $100 MILLION. IT'S KIND OF INTERESTING.

ONE OF THE THINGS ENTREPRENEURS GET UP THERE AND SAY IS, "WE HIT FOUR MILLION THIS MONTH," OR SOMETHING LIKE THAT. WELL, TO THE AVERAGE PERSON THAT'S COMPLETELY IRRELEVANT. WHAT DO THEY CARE WHETHER THE COMPANY HITS FOUR MILLION? WHAT IS THE EFFECT ON THEM? THE TRICK IS TO TRANSLATE THAT DOWN INTO THINGS THAT ARE IMPORTANT TO THEM, LIKE PROFIT SHARING.

WE ALSO TALK A LOT ABOUT FINANCIALS NOT BEING THE MOST IMPOR-TANT MEASURE. AT OUR COMPANY THE MOST IMPORTANT MEASURE IS GET-TING THE RIGHT THINGS DONE WELL. THAT'S OUR MEASURE OF SUCCESS; AND IT HAS TO DO WITH PRODUCTS AND SERVICES FOR THE END MARKET, AND IT HAS TO DO WITH BUILDING THE ORGANIZATION. AND WE REALLY FOCUS ON THOSE AS OUR MEASURES OF SUCCESS.

# PERSONAL TRANSITIONS REQUIRED

Taking on your four new roles of Team Builder, Coach, Planner, and Communicator, involves huge changes for you. You must learn new skills, break old habits, and apply your entrepreneurial strengths in new ways. What follows are the six transitions you will need to make in your leadership style as your company moves through Rapid Growth.

# GIVE AUTHORITY TO EXPERTS

Your focus must shift from supervising work done under your direct authority to assembling a team with its own authority and giving them the responsibility to direct and manage the work in their functional areas. You must hold the team accountable for producing results and operating in ways that are most productive for growing the company.

In Initial Growth, you started to delegate some decisions. You still have to make delegation a key component of your leadership style, but the delegating you do in Rapid Growth is very different. In Initial Growth, you delegated by dividing your role into different tasks and then supervising others to do things the way you would do them. You still made the ultimate decisions. Now you need to delegate authority to managers who have the expertise you lack so that they can make decisions and supervise their staff with far greater effectiveness than you would be able to do.

YOU HAVE TO GET THE HECK OUT OF THE WAY IF YOU'RE GOING TO LET SOMEONE GROW INTO A POSITION OF LEADERSHIP. YOU NEED TO PUT PEOPLE INTO A POSITION WHERE THE BUCK REALLY STOPS WITH THEM. TELL THEM, "THIS IS YOUR DEAL. IF YOU WANT TO HAVE A CONVERSATION ABOUT THE ALTERNATIVES, THEN LET'S HAVE THAT CONVERSATION. BUT DON'T COME TO ME AND ASK WHAT WE'RE GOING TO DO."

# USE A COLLABORATIVE STYLE

During Rapid Growth, you must ensure effective collaboration in your team and adopt a more consensus-oriented decision-making style. However, a collaborative style does not mean the team makes all the decisions. It's important to designate who "owns" decisions; most will belong to the functional leaders, some will belong to you, the company leader, and others need to be made by the whole team. In fact, you may still make many of the final decisions, but the difference is that you listen to everyone's input, help resolve disagreements, synthesize different views, and come up with a productive decision the team can accept and implement. Since the team is responsible for making sure the whole company buys into the decisions that are made, each member must be able to be a champion for all decisions (whether that person originally agreed with the idea or not). You make that much easier when you use a collaborative style and let the team play a significant role in reaching decisions.

THE MAIN POINT OF OUR MANAGEMENT MEETINGS IS TO REACH A CONSENSUS. A LOT OF PEOPLE MISUNDERSTAND WHAT THAT MEANS. IT'S NOT THE SAME AS

UNANIMOUS. IT MEANS THAT EVERYONE HAS INPUT, A DECISION GETS MADE, AND EVERYONE AGREES TO LIVE WITH THAT DECISION WITH FULL SUPPORT AND COMMITMENT—EVEN IF THERE WAS DISAGREEMENT AT FIRST.

You always want to be sure your team is part of and behind every important decision you make. This is a radical change from the leadership style you used in the earlier stages of the company's growth. Now, you cannot arrive in the morning and say, "This is what we're going to do," without having any discussion with your top management team. It's too dangerous. It separates your people from the decisions they must embrace, and it cuts you off from the information you need in order to avoid making bad decisions.

## FACILITATE EFFECTIVE TEAMWORK

There's only one way to build a team. First, make sure the members recognize and value each other's diverse styles and skills, build relationships, listen to each other, understand both shared and individual priorities, resolve conflicts, coordinate their work, and give each other feedback. Then tell them clearly that they have significant work to do *together as a team* to produce the plan for growth, monitor that plan, identify new initiatives, and communicate consistently to the staff. You need to facilitate the work of the team so that they can skillfully accomplish those tasks. That means you need to know when to step in and lead, and when to step back and let them lead.

> SUCCESS IN BUILDING MY TEAM HAS BEEN 80 PERCENT IN THE RECRUITING. I LOOK FOR SEVERAL THINGS: THEIR SKILL SET, THEIR VALUES AND HOW THEY WILL OPERATE, AND, VERY CANDIDLY, THAT PERSON'S EXPECTATIONS. I HAVE SOME FOLKS THAT I'VE HIRED THAT ASPIRE TO MY JOB OR ASPIRE TO THE CHIEF OPERATING OFFICER'S JOB IN OUR COMPANY, OR PERHAPS SOMEWHERE ELSE. THAT'S GREAT. THAT'S FINE TO KNOW. YOU WANT TO FIND THAT OUT DURING THE RECRUITING PROCESS. WE DO CROSS-FUNCTIONAL INTERVIEWING TO HELP US WITH THAT.
>
> THE OTHER 20 PERCENT IS IN THE "KOOL-AID®" THAT YOU FEED THEM ONCE THEY COME IN, MAKING SURE THAT THEY GET INVOLVED IN THE CULTURE OF THE ORGANIZATION AND THE STYLE OF THE MANAGEMENT TEAM VERY QUICKLY.

The collaborative style is very tough for some entrepreneurs to adopt. When you're used to operating independently, trying to work through a team and get them to do things can be very frustrating. You may need to work with a professional facilitator or executive coach to develop the skills required to lead the team and facilitate effective teamwork.

THERE ARE DAYS WHEN I THINK ENLIGHTENED DESPOTISM WOULD BE A SIM-
PLER WAY TO RUN THE BUSINESS. I MEAN, IT WOULD JUST BE QUICKER TO
ORDER IT DONE AND HAVE IT HAPPEN, RIGHT? BUT I'VE FOUND THAT'S A SHORT-
TERM BENEFIT; AND IF YOU WANT TO SURVIVE IN THE LONG RUN, YOU HAVE
TO BUILD A TEAM DYNAMIC WITHIN THE ORGANIZATION. IT DOESN'T JUST
HAPPEN. YOU HAVE TO WORK AT IT.

The trick is to consciously use techniques to keep your own impulses under control and ensure there are appropriate opportunities for your people to participate in the decision-making process.

IT TAKES A LOT OF WORK TO LEAD A TEAM. IT MEANS I HAVE TO BE
VULNERABLE. I HAVE TO THROW IDEAS ON THE TABLE THAT MIGHT NOT BE THE
BEST IDEAS IN THE WORLD, AND I HAVE TO BE ABLE TO TAKE VERY CANDID
FEEDBACK THAT TELLS ME THE IDEA IS AS DUMB AS DIRT. IT'S GOT TO BE OKAY
TO DO THAT. TEAMS ARE VERY PRECIOUS TO ORGANIZATIONS, BUT THEY TAKE
ALL OF THAT TO WORK WELL.

WHEN I GAVE UP THE IDEA THAT I WAS THE ONLY EXPERT IN THE ROOM, IT
FREED UP MY PEOPLE TO MAKE THEIR OWN DECISIONS AND TO PARTICIPATE
MORE IN THE DECISIONS WE HAD TO MAKE TOGETHER. IT MADE MEETINGS MUCH
MORE PRODUCTIVE, AND IT LIBERATED THE BUSINESS. IF I HAD CONTINUED THE
OLD WAY, MY COMPANY WOULD NOT BE GROWING.

THE MOST IMPORTANT THING I LEARNED TO DO AS WE GREW WAS REAL PLAN-
NING. BUT THE SECOND MOST IMPORTANT THING WAS TO DEVELOP SOME
TOOLS FOR RUNNING MEETINGS, TOOLS OF BRAINSTORMING SUCH AS FLIP
CHARTS, AND LOTS OF WAYS TO REALLY INVOLVE PEOPLE. THAT'S PROBABLY
THE MOST IMPORTANT FACTOR THAT HELPED US BUILD A HIGH-INVOLVEMENT
CULTURE, WHERE EVERYBODY IS INVOLVED IN MEETINGS AND IN DECISIONS.

Get past your frustrations and use the four keys to effective teamwork shown in the following box.

# VITAL SIGNS: KEYS TO EFFECTIVE TEAMWORK

**Manage your team as a group.** The "hub and spoke" style—with you in the middle and each team member directing communications only to you instead of to the team as a whole—may feel more comfortable, but it is extremely dangerous. It inhibits communication and coordination among the team. That's not the way to get team members to work together to fully leverage their skills and experience.

**Encourage teamwork through exchange of ideas with open feedback.** It's natural to dislike criticism, and it's difficult to avoid being defensive while you listen to others as they discuss your idea. But all team members, especially you, must learn how to overcome these feelings. It's your job to encourage everyone to hear all ideas, even the crazy ones (especially the crazy ones!) and to engage in healthy debate on company issues. Entrepreneurial leaders can show great leadership by seriously considering all ideas, even the critical ones, rather than cutting people off or trying to bury disagreement.

**Hold meetings you "love" (even though everybody hates meetings).** Learn to hold productive meetings, and you will wonder how you ever lived without them. Meetings facilitate working together as a team, developing plans, making decisions, and solving problems. If you think there's no time for meetings because you're moving so fast, then be prepared for major problems to arise. It is your job to schedule regular meetings, expect attendance, set the agenda, and manage the meeting so the time is productive. Separate strategic from operational meetings. Strategic issues rarely get prioritized as urgent; hence they tend to drop to the end of the agenda. Successful leaders usually have weekly team meetings for operational issues and monthly ones for strategic issues.

**Maintain alignment in the group.** It will be difficult for the team to stay aligned with the company's vision and goals, especially with so much going on at such a fast pace. But no matter how difficult it is, your number-one goal is to keep your team in alignment. If your team isn't in alignment, your people won't be in alignment, with the result that your company simply won't be able to grow to its potential.

I'VE ALWAYS TRIED HARD TO KEEP MY TEAM LINED UP AND FOCUSED ON COMMON GOALS. BUT AS WE GREW, I WAS SURPRISED TO FIND THERE WERE ASPECTS OF THE BUSINESS THAT EVERYONE AGREED TO ON THE SURFACE, BUT THEY WEREN'T REALLY ALIGNED. FOR EXAMPLE, I THOUGHT ALL SENIOR MANAGERS HAD BOUGHT INTO OUR SALES STRATEGY UNTIL WE HAD A MEETING WHERE THE VP OF PRODUCTS QUESTIONED ONE OF ITS FUNDAMENTAL PRINCIPLES IN FRONT OF A WHOLE ROOM FULL OF MANAGERS. HE CLEARLY DISAGREED WITH THE REST OF THE TEAM, AND HAVING IT COME OUT SO BLATANTLY IN FRONT OF EVERYONE CAUSED A LOT OF CONFUSION. DISAGREEMENT IS FINE WHEN THE STRATEGY IS BEING DEVELOPED OR APPEARS OFF-TRACK, BUT HE NEVER BROUGHT UP HIS ISSUES UNTIL MUCH LATER—AND THEN HE DID SO IN PUBLIC. I REALIZED PART OF THE PROBLEM WAS HIS PROBLEM: HE WAS FOCUSED PRIMARILY ON HIS AREA OF PRODUCTS. BUT THE OTHER PART OF THE PROBLEM WAS MY PROBLEM: I HADN'T REALIZED HOW IMPORTANT IT WAS TO GET HIS AGREEMENT WITH SUCH A MAJOR STRATEGY. MY LESSON: DON'T ASSUME YOU HAVE ALIGNMENT; CHECK IT REGULARLY.

I THINK IT'S IMPORTANT TO GIVE TEAM MEMBERS OPPORTUNITIES TO GET INVOLVED WITH EACH OTHER. WE HAVE AN ANNUAL OFF-SITE EVERY SUMMER. THIS YEAR I HAD A LONGER OFF-SITE THAN I NORMALLY WOULD HAVE. AND THE TIMING WAS A LITTLE BIT DIFFERENT AND A LITTLE EARLIER BECAUSE I'D JUST BROUGHT ALL THOSE NEW PEOPLE IN, AND I WANTED US TO HAVE TO DEAL WITH EACH OTHER OVER AN EXTENDED PERIOD OF TIME. THAT HELPED QUITE A BIT.

AND ODDS ARE, SOMETHING'S NOT GOING TO WORK OUT VERY WELL. SOMETHING'S NOT GOING TO BE PERFECT. BUT I THINK IF YOU AS THE CEO KEEP WORKING AT THAT AND KEEP ENCOURAGING THE COMMUNICATION AND OFFER CLARITY ABOUT YOUR EXPECTATIONS, ABOUT PERFORMANCE AS WELL AS BEHAVIOR, THAT YOU HAVE A GOOD CHANCE OF HAVING IT WORK OUT REASONABLY WELL.

## BECOME THE CHIEF PLANNER AND COMMUNICATOR

Making a plan and communicating the plan are the best ways to keep your management and employees aligned and focused.

## The plan and the planning process

The plan tells the team members what the priorities are and what they are supposed to be doing with their days. Every individual should know the plan and be part of it, and be responsible for following it. Once you break the habit of thinking of a *plan* as a four-letter word, you will learn to use both the planning process and the plan itself as tools for growth. In fact, the experience of planning is as important as the actual plan you create because the process enables people to become accustomed to raising issues and choosing among options. Thus, creating the shared mission and vision, with the accompanying 12- to 24-month plan, helps build the team and strengthens its ability to stay aligned. As the leader, you need to drive this process.

I WAS A CLUELESS ENTREPRENEUR WHO KNEW NOTHING ABOUT BUSINESS OR BUILDING A COMPANY. WE WENT ALONG FINE, GROWING REVENUES NICELY FOR SEVERAL YEARS UNTIL WE REALIZED THAT WE HAD TO LEARN HOW TO PLAN IF WE WANTED TO KEEP GROWING. UP TO THEN WE DID NO PLANNING. MAYBE THAT'S HARD TO BELIEVE THAT WE HAD ABSOLUTELY NO PLANNING, BUT THAT'S WHAT WE DID. I'M AN ENGINEER. I FOUND PLANNING IS SORT OF A FOUR-LETTER WORD AMONG TECHNICAL PEOPLE. THEY JUST DON'T WANT TO PLAN. THEY DON'T LIKE DOING IT. THEY'RE NOT GOOD AT IT. IT MEANS INVOLVING THE FUTURE. THE FUTURE IS UNCERTAIN. SO WE LEARNED A FRAMEWORK FOR PLANNING WHICH WAS REALLY IMPORTANT IN TERMS OF GETTING ALIGNMENT WITHIN THE COMPANY. WE WERE AT A POINT WHERE SUDDENLY NOT EVERYBODY KNEW WHAT WE WERE DOING, AND THIS IS A WAY TO GET EVERYBODY UNDERSTANDING THE PURPOSE OF THE COMPANY. WE WENT THROUGH A FAIRLY FORMAL PROCESS, WHICH WAS QUITE SUCCESSFUL.

But be careful of the type of plan you develop: Many plans are all numbers and simply tell people, "In this quarter, we'll make this much money and we'll spend this much money." It may also have a personnel component, such as "We'll hire 30 new people." But all too often, plans do not include goals. You must have specific, clear goals: "We're going to reduce the competitive power of XYZ Corp., and here's how we're going to do it." Only when the plan states just what you intend to do to make your business successful can you call it a plan.

YOU, THE CEO, ARE RESPONSIBLE FOR MORE THAN THE VISION; YOU'RE RESPONSIBLE FOR THE EFFECTIVE EXECUTION OF THE GAME PLAN. AND I THINK IT'S IMPORTANT TO SHARE EVEN THE SMALL SUCCESSES. THE ORGANIZATION NEEDS TO FEEL THAT IT'S ACHIEVING ITS GOALS. SO SHARING THOSE SUCCESSES AND THE PROGRESS IS CRITICAL.

## COMMUNICATING THE MESSAGE
## THROUGH DIFFERENT MEDIA

You must also become the leader for all company communications, using various methods to explain the vision, plans, goals, issues, decisions, and news. Everyone in the company wants to hear from you, their leader, about what's going on in the company, what the future looks like, what you expect of them, and what's going on in your head. Your job is to find the most productive ways to meet this seemingly impossible demand. You can and should do a lot of communicating through your managers, but you yourself must take on the responsibility of doing whatever it takes to keep the company fully informed, focused, and directed so everyone can be proactive and productive.

I HAD A FEW TECHNIQUES FOR STAYING CLOSE THAT WORKED PRETTY WELL AS THE COMPANY GREW. WALKING AROUND THE BUILDING AND DROPPING INTO PEOPLE'S OFFICES DID NOT WORK FOR ME. NUMBER ONE, BY THE TIME I GET TO THE OFFICE, I HAVE A WHOLE DAY OF MEETINGS SCHEDULED. AND I WON'T MAKE THE TIME. PLUS, I FOUND THAT PEOPLE DON'T REALLY LIKE IT WHEN THEY'RE DOING SOMETHING AND YOU DROP IN ON THEM. I MEAN, IT'S NICE WHEN THE PRESIDENT PAYS ATTENTION, BUT IT'S SORT OF AWKWARD, TOO. SO I ORGANIZED SOMETHING CALLED "DONUTS WITH DOUG." I WOULD COME IN AND BRING DONUTS ON FRIDAY MORNINGS. THERE WAS NO AGENDA. EVERYONE WAS INVITED. AND I NEVER KNEW WHO WOULD SHOW UP OR WHAT THE TOPIC WOULD BE. IT'S USUALLY SOMETHING CURRENT. PEOPLE RAISE THEIR ISSUES. IT WAS A GOOD MECHANISM FOR RESPONDING TO EMPLOYEES, BUT IT DIDN'T GET ME THE FEEDBACK I WANTED. SO I SET UP REGULAR LUNCHES WITH RANDOMLY SELECTED GROUPS. THOSE WERE REALLY INTERESTING, BUT I HAD TO BE CAREFUL. IT DIDN'T WORK FOR SOMEONE TO RAISE AN ISSUE AND THEN FOR ME TO GO RUNNING DOWN TO THE VICE PRESIDENT'S OFFICE ASKING WHAT HE WAS DOING ABOUT IT. THAT IS NOT EFFECTIVE. BUT TALKING ABOUT THE COMPANY'S VISION AND GOALS, LISTENING, AND FINDING SOME WAY TO PURSUE SERIOUS ISSUES WAS MY CHARTER.

How do you know when you are communicating well? When you and the people around you have a deep and shared understanding of the company and its goals. Few things are more disturbing for a leader than to realize that people around you don't know what they should know. This is frustrating, especially when the information or issues are so clear and obvious to you. Leaders often feel they have repeated these topics many times, yet people still don't seem to "get it."

Such feelings are warning signs that you aren't communicating adequately. It's impossible to overcommunicate. An iterative process—in which you describe and explain, then listen to people's responses, and then explain more and solicit their concerns and ideas—works best.

Helping people internalize information is hard, but it will take less effort from you and your managers if people are truly involved in the planning, problem-solving, and decision-making processes. When your company is set up to enable this kind of participation and input, people absorb information much faster and increase their ability and motivation to execute accordingly.

> MY BEST SKILL IS TO COMMUNICATE AND PULL IDEAS AND OPPORTUNITIES OUT OF OTHER PEOPLE. I SEE THAT AS MY FUNCTION IN THE COMPANY. IT'S MY JOB TO BUILD INTERNAL AND EXTERNAL RELATIONSHIPS SO THERE IS POSITIVE COMMUNICATION THROUGHOUT THE ORGANIZATION AND WITH OUR CUSTOMERS.

You may have difficulty finding time for all this communication, but you can't afford not to do it. If you don't, people get distracted and revert to reactive fire-fighting and wheel-spinning, with few tangible results. Don't wait to work on this focused communication until you have some kind of crisis. The hardest time to create the laser-beam focus and get everyone aligned behind it is during the chaos of a crisis. Your challenge and opportunity is to be the chief communicator, the one who organizes and maintains that focus at all times.

> YOU HAVE TO HAVE A GAME PLAN, AND IT HAS TO HAVE ACHIEVABLE OBJECTIVES. THE OBJECTIVES HAVE TO BE MEASURABLE, TOO. AND YOU HAVE TO MEASURE THEM AND REPORT BACK ON THEM. THERE'S NOTHING WORSE THAN SETTING UP A BUNCH OF OBJECTIVES, MOVING ON, AND NEVER COMING BACK TO THEM. NOBODY KNOWS WHETHER YOU DID THE THINGS YOU SET OUT TO DO.
>
> WHEN YOU'RE GROWING AND CHANGING, YOU HAVE TO REPORT BACK TO YOUR EMPLOYEES ON A VERY STEADY BASIS. "HERE'S WHAT WE SAID WE WOULD DO. HERE'S WHAT WE DID." OR "WE MISSED THIS ONE, BUT HERE'S WHAT WE'RE GOING TO DO INSTEAD." YOU'VE GOT TO BE HONEST WITH YOURSELF, AND YOU'VE GOT TO BE HONEST WITH THE TEAM.

## FIX ORGANIZATIONAL MISFITS

During this stage, you must pay close attention to the organization and how all the people and processes fit together to support Rapid Growth. One of the most difficult challenges is to fix organizational problems that result from growth. As the scopes of the various jobs expand, some of the people you first hired are no longer competent or able to fill their roles. You must move them into jobs with levels of responsibility that match their abilities or provide an opportunity for them to leave with dignity.

A LOT OF PEOPLE WE HIRED, PEOPLE I LOVE TREMENDOUSLY, HAVE FALLEN BY THE WAYSIDE OVER THE YEARS AT THE COMPANY. IT'S THE ONES WHO KEPT ON LEARNING WHO HAVE GROWN WITH THE COMPANY, THE ONES WHO TAKE THE INITIATIVE TO NETWORK AND READ BUSINESS BOOKS AND SUBSCRIBE TO THE *WALL STREET JOURNAL*. THEY HAVE A CONSTANT STREAM OF NEW INFORMATION COMING IN, AND THEY KEEP LEARNING AND GROWING WITH THE JOB. AND THAT'S THE ONLY SUCCESS FACTOR I CAN THINK OF THAT'S SUSTAINABLE OVER THE LONG TERM—THE DESIRE AND ABILITY TO KEEP LEARNING.

At the same time, you may have hired new people whom you discover don't fit the company's needs. If the problem is a deficiency in skills, you can try training them, but that takes time. If they fit the culture and values and are highly motivated to learn new skills, spending the time to train them may be worth it. But if they don't fit the company's culture or values, they need to leave.

YOU HAVE TO HIRE THE RIGHT PEOPLE WHO HIRE THE RIGHT PEOPLE WHO HIRE THE RIGHT PEOPLE. IF PEOPLE ARE NOT PHILOSOPHICALLY ALIGNED TO YOUR VALUE SET, YOU CAN'T CHANGE THEM. A LOT OF PEOPLE HIRE JUST BASED ON SKILLS. SKILLS ARE THE LEAST-IMPORTANT THING. I CAN TEACH PEOPLE SKILLS. I JUST CAN'T TEACH THEM TO HAVE A SET OF VALUES.

The worst situation is when people have terrific skills but don't fit the values. You must recognize these situations as quickly as possible, explain to them that it's not going to work out, and get them out of the company. Letting people like this stay too long harms your culture more than you realize. If you don't take action in such situations, this signals to everyone else that the culture and values aren't that important to you. The misfits will infect others, especially if they are in management positions. Even though admitting a hiring mistake is hard, it must be done with enough objectivity to show that mistakes are inevitable and that they're okay if you can turn them into lessons for the future.

ONE OF OUR BIGGEST PROBLEMS WAS NOT FIRING PEOPLE SOON ENOUGH, NOT REALIZING THAT WE HAD HIRED WRONG IN THE FIRST PLACE. IT'S EASY TO COMPOUND THAT MISTAKE, TOLERATING THE PERSONAL AGENDAS OF PROBLEM PEOPLE AS WELL AS THEIR LACK OF FIT WITH OUR VALUES AND CULTURE AND, EVEN WORSE, NOT REALIZING THE EFFECT OF THEIR WEAKNESSES AND MEDIOCRITY ON THE WHOLE COMPANY. YOU HAVE TO BE SURE THERE IS A PROBLEM; BUT ONCE YOU ARE, BETTER TO BITE THE BULLET AND MAKE THE HARD CHOICES THAN TO SUFFER THE DAMAGE THE WRONG PEOPLE CAN DO.

WE LOST FOCUS ON VALUES. WE THOUGHT OUR VALUES AND OUR CULTURE WERE THE MOST IMPORTANT THING, BUT THEN WE JUST KIND OF LOST SIGHT OF THEM. ORIGINALLY WHEN WE HIRED, WE INTERVIEWED 12 PEOPLE FOR EACH JOB AND CHECKED CAREFULLY FOR CULTURAL FIT. AS WE GREW LARGER AND MORE COMPLACENT, WE STARTED BRINGING IN PEOPLE WHO HAD CERTAIN SETS OF SKILLS REGARDLESS OF THEIR UNDERLYING PHILOSOPHY. SO WHAT DID WE GET? WE GOT PEOPLE WHO HAD THEIR OWN AGENDAS AND JUST DIDN'T FIT OUR VALUES AT ALL. WE WOULD INTERVIEW SOMEBODY, AND THEY WOULD BE HIRED SO THE COMPETITORS WOULDN'T GET THEM. ONCE YOU START HIRING THIS WAY, ESPECIALLY MANAGEMENT, YOU'RE DOOMED. YOU CAN'T BREAK OUT OF THE CYCLE. BECAUSE YOU START HIRING MANAGERS WHO AREN'T ALIGNED, AREN'T INVOLVED, WHO HAVE THEIR OWN AGENDAS. AND THEN THEY START BRINGING IN PEOPLE WHO GENERALLY ARE MORE LOYAL TO THEM THAN TO THE COMPANY. EVEN WORSE THAN THAT, THE MANAGERS TENDED TO BRING IN PEOPLE WHO WERE NOT EVEN AS GOOD AS THEY WERE. SO WE GOT PEOPLE WHO WERE NOT ALIGNED AND NOT SKILLED, AND WE FAILED—BIG TIME.

# BE A PROCESS CHAMPION

In Rapid Growth, one of the company's chief goals is to standardize and streamline processes and systems for effective decision making and efficient work flow in every functional area. Some entrepreneurs resist imposing these standard practices, believing that doing so will make their company too bureaucratic. But if you don't define and develop some standard operating procedures, people will have to reinvent the wheel for every situation. Your role is to make sure your processes and systems are efficient and helpful, well understood, followed appropriately, and coordinated across all functions. Successful entrepreneurs understand how to embed the mission, vision, and values of the company into the whole organization. They create an infrastructure that supports growth by developing reliable and consistent processes, policies, and systems in several key areas listed below.

## PROCESSES FOR MANAGING AND LEADING PEOPLE

- Attracting, recruiting, selecting, and hiring people
- Orienting and integrating them into the company
- Managing performance and developing people by providing opportunities for continuous learning
- Delegating without abdicating

- Developing a team

- Compensating people (rewards and recognition)

- Promoting and advancing people, succession planning

- Retiring people

- Terminating people

## PROCESSES FOR PLANNING AND ALIGNMENT

- Planning

- Tracking customer and market information

- Continuous improvement/innovation

- Communications up, down, and across the company

- Developing metrics, measurement, and feedback

- Organizational development and team building

- Aligning individual goals with company goals

- Meeting facilitation and management

## PROCESSES FOR MANAGEMENT AND CONTROL

- Budgeting

- Information management and communications technology

- Tracking revenue, expense, and profitability

- Facilities and equipment needed to support productivity

## PROCESSES FOR SALES AND MARKETING

- Lead qualification

- Pipeline management

- Sales targets

- New market development

- Market launch

- Customer feedback

## PROCESSES FOR PRODUCTION

- Inventory control
- Manufacturing and production
- Quality management
- Shipping and delivery
- Customer support

Without these processes in place, the company will not be able to survive the demands of Rapid Growth; it's that simple and that critical.

> I HAVE DONE A LOT IN MY ORGANIZATION TO FORCE ADHERENCE TO PROCESSES, ESPECIALLY CROSS-FUNCTIONAL KINDS OF COLLABORATION, TO THE POINT WHERE THERE ARE MEETINGS THAT I REFUSE TO HAVE OR THAT I REFUSE TO PARTICIPATE IN IF THERE AREN'T PEOPLE PRESENT FROM DIFFERENT DEPARTMENTS (FOR EXAMPLE, FROM ENGINEERING AND MARKETING). WE'VE CREATED SOME STRUCTURE AND PROCESS THAT FORCE SOME OF THE INTER-DISCIPLINARY OR CROSS-FUNCTIONAL KINDS OF STUFF TO HAPPEN. IN THE EARLY STAGE, THIS HAPPENED NATURALLY, BUT NOW I FIND I MUST CON-SCIOUSLY AND EXPLICITLY PUSH PEOPLE FROM DIFFERENT AREAS TO SOLVE PROBLEMS TOGETHER. AS THE CEO, THERE ARE A LOT OF THE THINGS THAT YOU HAVE TO PUSH TO MAKE HAPPEN. SOMETIMES YOU HAVE TO FORCE THEM TO HAPPEN. AND YOU SHOULD NOT TOLERATE BEHAVIOR THAT ISN'T CON-STRUCTIVE IN THAT REGARD.
>
> YOU ALSO HAVE TO BE REALLY CAREFUL THAT YOU DON'T CHEAT ON THOSE KINDS OF ISSUES YOURSELF. PEOPLE PAY A LOT OF ATTENTION TO WHAT YOU *DO* AS CEO. IF YOU START TO WORK ON AN ISSUE WITH ONE PART OF THE ORGANIZATION AND ANOTHER PART OF THE ORGANIZATION REALLY NEEDS TO BE PART OF THAT PROCESS, AND IT BECOMES CLEAR THAT YOU'RE WORKING AROUND THAT PROCESS, OR YOU'RE WORKING AROUND THOSE ORGANIZATIONS, THEN 23 LECTURES ABOUT HOW IMPORTANT IT IS TO DO IT THE RIGHT WAY DON'T REALLY MATTER. SO YOU'VE GOT TO BE REALLY, REALLY CAREFUL ABOUT THE WAY YOU BEHAVE YOURSELF.

# HABITS TO BREAK

Changing your manner and style of leadership is not easy. If you've grown to this point, you've already broken the bad habits of Initial Growth: micromanaging, resisting plans and processes, and undisciplined decision making. Now you need to change two other habits.

## ASSUMING EVERYONE IN THE COMPANY IS LIKE YOU

It's easy to fall into the trap of unconsciously believing that others think the way you do, want to operate the same way, experience the same frustrations, and have the same perspectives. As you add more people to the company, it's essential to realize that each person adds a unique set of strengths and characteristics. To encourage the best performance, your managers need to understand each person's goals and motivations and help each to achieve his or her objectives. The more successful you can be in stepping into others' shoes, treating them the way you'd like to be treated, and understanding and valuing their ideas and contributions, the more you can engage them in creating a shared vision for growth and turning that vision into reality.

> RECOGNIZE THAT YOU'RE DEVELOPING LEADERS, NOT CLONES OF YOUR LEADERSHIP. YOUR JOB IS TO DEVELOP PEOPLE WHO CAN LEAD IN A SUCCESSFUL DIRECTION.

## THINKING YOU MUST HAVE ALL THE ANSWERS AND BE THE CREATIVE ONE

In the early days, you had all the vision, ideas, and answers. It was your creativity that drove growth. Now you must admit that you don't have all the answers and that more—sometimes better—ideas will come from others. Once you actively solicit ideas, others are freed up and truly empowered to contribute their creativity.

> YOU PROVIDE THE ENVIRONMENT, AND THEN THEY EITHER BECOME LEADERS OR THEY DON'T. IF THEY'RE THE ONES YOU WANT IN THOSE POSITIONS, THEY WILL TAKE ADVANTAGE OF THE ENVIRONMENT AND SIMPLY DO IT. IF THEY DON'T, THEY'RE SIMPLY NOT THE LEADERS YOU'RE LOOKING FOR.

# APPLYING YOUR ENTREPRENEURIAL SKILLS

During Rapid Growth, you continue to apply your entrepreneurial strengths—such as seeing the vision and new possibilities, thinking out of the box, being a creative idea generator—and you use your love of learning to add new skills in planning, team building, communication, and coaching. This combination of old and new skills enables you to better understand people and better know how to leverage their ideas. You stimulate a whole new kind of creativity and entrepreneurial spirit throughout the organization.

This creativity comes not just from you, but also from the synergy of having many people aggressively searching for new opportunities to achieve the shared vision and searching for novel ways to improve the company's products, processes, and ability to achieve its goals. You've always been the creative entrepreneur; now you can use this strength to encourage the kind of companywide creativity and innovation required for the next stage of growth: Continuous Growth.

I HAVE A METAPHOR FOR THE CEO'S ROLE: A PILOT. IF HE (OR SHE) IS ACTIVELY FLYING THE PLANE HIMSELF, HE DOESN'T HAVE A LOT OF RESERVE. SO WHEN THINGS START TO GO HAYWIRE, WHEN PROBLEMS OR CHANGES IN THE ENVIRONMENT OCCUR, HE CAN GET OVERLOADED VERY QUICKLY. SO IF YOU ARE HAND-FLYING YOUR ORGANIZATION, YOU NEED TO CREATE A MECHANISM THAT WILL ALLOW YOU TO PULL BACK A LITTLE BIT, SO YOU HAVE SOME RESERVE AND SOME PERSPECTIVE. BECAUSE I HAVE AN AUTOPILOT (ANALOGOUS TO MY MANAGEMENT TEAM), I HAVE TIME TO LOOK AT THE RADAR SCREEN. I DON'T HAVE TO SPEND ALL MY TIME FOCUSED ON THE INSTRUMENTS. THAT MEANS I HAVE TIME TO IDENTIFY THE BUMPS AHEAD. A CEO INVOLVED IN THE EVERYDAY OPERATIONS OF THE BUSINESS MAY NOT HAVE THE PERSPECTIVE OR THE RESERVE TO DEAL WITH THE CHANGE ISSUES THAT COME UP IN OUR VERY, VERY RAPIDLY CHANGING ENVIRONMENT.

FOR SEVERAL YEARS, WE WERE JUST TRYING TO STAY ALIVE. WE WERE BASICALLY DRIVEN TOWARD THE NEXT OPPORTUNITY THAT WOULD PUT SOME MONEY INTO THE BANK AND ALLOW US TO BUILD THE BUSINESS. SO IT WAS A VERY SALES-DRIVEN ORGANIZATION, WITHOUT A LOT OF FOCUS ON MARKET POSITIONING, MARKETING STRATEGY, AND DISTRIBUTION STRATEGY. NOT THAT BEING OPPORTUNITY-DRIVEN IS A BAD THING. SOMETIMES, IT'S EXACTLY WHAT YOU HAVE TO DO. BUT IT DOESN'T SCALE INDEFINITELY. SO AT A CERTAIN POINT, GETTING CLEAR ON STRATEGY, PRIORITIES, AND POSITIONING BECAME CRITICAL GOALS IF WE REALLY WANTED TO GROW AND COMPETE MORE SUCCESSFULLY. ONCE WE SAW THIS, WE PULLED OUT OF REACTIVE MODE AND STARTED ADDING THE RIGHT KINDS OF EXPERTISE. WE HIRED A VP OF MARKETING, A VP OF INFORMATION TECHNOLOGY, AND A VP OF HUMAN RESOURCES—ALL TO COVER IMPORTANT FUNCTIONS THAT JUST WEREN'T BEING COVERED. WE HAD TO BUILD THE INFRASTRUCTURE THAT WE WERE MISSING BECAUSE NOT HAVING IT MADE US LAG BEHIND AND STUNTED OUR GROWTH.

# SUMMARY:
# RAPID GROWTH STAGE

## COMPANY GOALS

- Gain significant market share as products become widely used.
- Become a market leader and ward off competitors.
- Build infrastructure and management team to support aggressive growth.
- Hire and integrate a lot of new people.

## COMPANY CHARACTERISTICS

- Competition heats up and customers grow more demanding; there's huge pressure to deliver more.
- Tension between the need to move fast versus the need to build structure, plans, and systems.
- Staff and management grow quickly and become more diverse.
- Business is market focused.
- Planning begins and people work to the plan.
- Operations start to be standardized and streamlined.
- Expectations of the company from all constituencies are huge.
- The fast pace is extreme.

## RED FLAGS: SIGNALS FOR CHANGING YOUR ROLE

- Feel pressure to fill voids in company's functional expertise.
- See the need to build your management team's ability to streamline and coordinate their functions and work together as a team to plan for the future.

*cont...*

-CONTINUED

- Want to be more proactive, but hard to find time.

- Always feel behind the curve.

- Hard to keep the original culture as new people are added.

- Best way to fund growth is unclear.

- Some original employees can't keep pace with growing responsibilities.

- You realize how easy it would be to lose control.

## DANGERS IF YOU DON'T CHANGE

- Functional silos, office politics, and even infighting will develop.

- People will complain about having too many priorities and spending all their time fighting fires; they will lose touch with vision, strategy, and goals. People will think that the culture and values aren't important to you.

- Products will begin to look tired; competitors will start to bite at your heels.

- Lack of structure and process will create delays; it will be too hard to get things done.

- People won't feel empowered and will feel they are spinning their wheels.

- The company will lose focus and won't be able to grow.

- Decline.

### KEY LEADERSHIP ROLES

- Team Builder
- Coach
- Planner
- Communicator

### CRITICAL RESPONSIBILITIES

- Hire people who are smarter than you to fill gaps in functional expertise.
- Help management team work together productively with mutual trust.
- Define new roles/responsibilities and goals for management team.
- Lead team in creating a strategic market-focused vision and plan for growth and in following it.
- Create processes to continually align employees—especially the management team—with company's vision and culture.
- Drive a meaningful communication process, including being a champion for market and customer information and communication.
- Listen to and consider views of all constituencies.

*cont...*

-CONTINUED

## PERSONAL CHANGES TO MAKE IN YOUR LEADERSHIP ROLE

- Use the company's plan to focus and track its efforts.

- Shift your focus from doing work to managing and coaching others.

- Stop being the ultimate decision maker in every area; develop a consensus-oriented decision-making style and capitalize on your team's abilities.

- Learn to facilitate effective teamwork; hold team meetings more frequently than one-on-one discussions.

- Encourage all ideas to be heard in a healthy debate that allows for criticism.

- Stop tolerating organizational misfits.

- Admit you don't have all the answers or ideas; focus on unleashing the creativity of others.

- Be a champion for effective, efficient processes.

- Consciously balance your time, working equally between the big picture and daily operations.

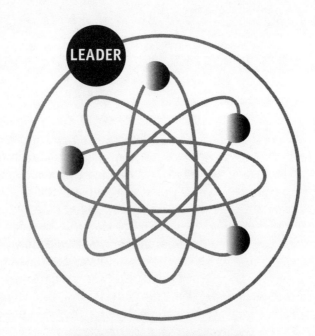

**CONTINUOUS GROWTH**

**Change Catalyst**
**Organization Builder**
**Strategic Innovator**
**Chief of Culture**

# CHAPTER 4

# CONTINUOUS GROWTH

We had always been a consensus-driven company, but when we decided on a new strategic direction, there was much less consensus than usual. I always tried to bring the management team together and make decisions in unison. But we had reached a new stage of growth, and everybody had different theories on how to handle it. The marketing guy saw one set of problems; the sales VP saw another. It slowed down our decision making just when we needed to make decisions more quickly. When that happens, you learn that it's up to you to pull back and make the big-picture decisions. You have to define the new directions. You've got to look people in the eye and say, "This is the decision. This is the direction we're going to go in. Either you're with the program or you need to leave." It may not be comfortable, but it's what the organization needs at that point. You, the CEO, must convey the sense of urgency and your commitment and dedication to the company's success in pursuing the new direction.

## YOUR COMPANY'S NEW GOALS IN CONTINUOUS GROWTH

In Chapter 3 we discussed Rapid Growth and the need to build the management team, share leadership with them, and develop the organization's internal processes and structure. You learned that success in this stage results in more customers and market opportunities, a much larger employee base, and a more complex organization. But once again you'll need to change your formula for success and your management style in order to realize the potential of Continuous Growth. You'll have to do the following in order to grow:

- Find new markets.

- Grow new niches in the current market.

- Expand product lines.

- Provide more "total solutions" to help customers.

- Brand the company and its people as thought leaders.

Achieving these new goals might include these strategies:

- New product development

- Strategic alliances

- Acquisitions or mergers

- Spinning off a subsidiary (that may even cannibalize the core business)

- Significant funding with an IPO and/or corporate partnerships

Any of these new strategies will demand drastic changes in the company's way of operating. At the same time, the company must handle a set of problems that can create significant turbulence: increased customer demands, new competitive threats, technology changes, investor pressures, and possibly an internal infrastructure that is not strong enough or no longer operates efficiently. Since the company has added more and more employees, it may be difficult for the management team to keep track of all parts of the company. You, the CEO, must focus on developing, then implementing, new organizational strategies that will enable everyone to stay aligned.

To remain on the leading edge of the industry and achieve the goals of Continuous Growth, you and your management team must reduce this turbulence and adopt a new way of thinking about the company. You must fundamentally transform the way it operates. This means defining a new vision, determining what needs to change to achieve this vision, and creating a new formula for success (see the following figure).

This period is a critical turning point for the company and for you as leader. Many entrepreneurs allow their companies to become victims of the turbulence by holding on too

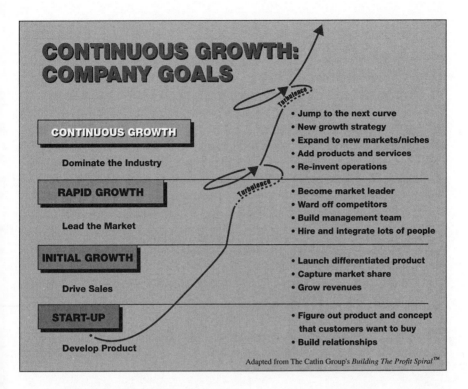

**CONTINUOUS GROWTH: COMPANY GOALS**

| | |
|---|---|
| **CONTINUOUS GROWTH** | • Jump to the next curve |
| | • New growth strategy |
| | • Expand to new markets/niches |
| Dominate the Industry | • Add products and services |
| | • Re-invent operations |
| **RAPID GROWTH** | • Become market leader |
| | • Ward off competitors |
| | • Build management team |
| Lead the Market | • Hire and integrate lots of people |
| **INITIAL GROWTH** | • Launch differentiated product |
| | • Capture market share |
| Drive Sales | • Grow revenues |
| **START-UP** | • Figure out product and concept that customers want to buy |
| Develop Product | • Build relationships |

Adapted from The Catlin Group's *Building The Profit Spiral*™

long to old operational methods, without realizing they are no longer sustainable. The more proactive you are in leading the required transformation, the healthier your growth path will be. The key to success is to transform sooner rather than later.

In addition to this initial transformation, the Continuous Growth stage requires *continual transformations* (as often as every 12 to 36 months) to take advantage of emerging opportunities and to remain an industry leader.

## RED FLAGS: WARNING SIGNS THAT TELL YOU IT'S TIME TO CHANGE ROLES

As you enter Continuous Growth, you will again notice red flags popping up all around you, indications that your leadership role needs to change once more. Moving into Continuous Growth can feel like flying through a thunderhead. The

*cont...*

*-continued*

turbulence keeps increasing even as you're successfully riding the ramp of Rapid Growth. Here are some of the red flags that tell you you're entering the Continuous Growth stage:

 You need to spend most of your time outside the company, building external relationships, finding strategic partners, being a spokesperson, talking with analysts, and doing road shows to raise money. But you don't know whether your management team can run the business for very long without having you there.

 You are frustrated that no one seems to have the same sense of urgency about the future as you do. You see a lot of changes in the external environment and recognize many of the problems and opportunities they represent. But you're the only one thinking about the big picture; everyone else is focusing on the here and now.

 You've added so many people that the organization feels unwieldy. You want to reorganize but aren't sure what will work best.

 Other people are getting frustrated, asking basic questions like, "Where are we going, anyway?" They're complaining that the right hand doesn't know what the left hand is doing.

 Your role as CEO keeps expanding, and you feel like you're "cheating" on all aspects of it, with way too many people and decisions dependent on you and not enough time to focus. You wonder whether you need a COO.

 One or more members of your management team are driving you crazy.

 You feel as if you're communicating all the time, but people aren't "getting it." Managers complain about the decision-making process and say decisions are not clear.

 Your people don't feel empowered, but you're frustrated because you don't think you're micromanaging.

You can see new strategic opportunities to maximize growth, but they'll require big changes and you don't want people to think you're just being the "crazy entrepreneur" who isn't focused enough. You're worried about throwing the entire company into turmoil.

 You're seriously considering an IPO or a big acquisition, but you're worried about what that will do to the culture of your company.

 You want to figure out how to keep the culture entrepreneurial and "small" as the company grows, but it seems impossible. People are just not acting in accord with the values that everyone shared when the company was smaller.

 You're worried that people you count on and want to keep might leave the company.

 Just as you whack down one problem, another one pops up, just as difficult and serious—and it's hard to get people to help you deal with these problems.

WE'VE MADE THREE OR FOUR SMALL ACQUISITIONS OVER THE COURSE OF THE LAST COUPLE OF YEARS, TECHNOLOGY AND CORPORATE ACQUISITIONS. THE SMALL ONES WERE REALLY EASY. WE JUST ABSORBED THEM INTO THE COMPANY. THAT WAS NO PROBLEM. THEN WE MADE A BIG ONE LAST YEAR. AND WE HAVE REQUIRED MASSIVE DOSES OF PEPTO-BISMOL TO DIGEST THAT ACQUISITION. IT REALLY HAS ACCELERATED A TRANSFORMATION IN THE COMPANY THAT WE INTENDED TO GO THROUGH, BUT I THINK WE DIDN'T REALIZE JUST HOW LARGE AND HOW DIFFICULT THAT WAS GOING TO BE.

I ALWAYS THOUGHT I COULD RUN ANY BUSINESS, BUT WHEN WE GOT REALLY BIG, THE JOY WAS GONE FOR ME. I WOULD SPEND MY DAYS VISITING CUSTOMERS BECAUSE THAT'S WHAT I LIKED TO DO, BUT OUR PLANNING SUFFERED. I DIDN'T RECOGNIZE THE CHANGES I NEEDED TO MAKE. I ALMOST LOST THE

COMPANY BEFORE I REALIZED THAT I WAS THE PROBLEM AND HAD TO MAKE SOME RADICAL CHANGES IN THE WAY I WORKED.

WHEN WE WERE SMALL, I LOOKED AT ALL THE PLANS FOR ALL OF THE AREAS OF THE BUSINESS AND MADE SURE THEY ALL WORKED TOGETHER. WHEN WE GOT TO AROUND 100 PEOPLE, THAT BECAME TOO HARD TO DO. SO I HAD THE EXECUTIVE MANAGEMENT TEAM LOOK AT ALL THE PLANS AND MAKE SURE THEY WORKED. AND THEN WE GOT TO 150 PEOPLE AND THERE WAS JUST TOO MUCH GOING ON. WE WOULD HAVE THESE ALL-DAY MEETINGS TO REVIEW ALL THE PLANS, AND WOULD FIND THAT FOR EVERY 10 PEOPLE ON THE MANAGEMENT TEAM, THERE WERE ONLY TWO THAT WOULD UNDERSTAND ANY GIVEN PART OF THE PLAN. IT WOULD BE OUTSIDE THE EXPERTISE OF THE OTHER EIGHT. IT WAS OVERWHELMING FOR ME BECAUSE EVEN THOUGH I KNEW ALL THE DIFFERENT SPOTS, I DIDN'T HAVE DEPTH IN ALL OF THEM. I STARTED TO FEEL WE WERE GETTING OUT OF CONTROL. SO WE DEVELOPED A NEW WAY OF WORKING. WE LET GO OF THE HIERARCHY, SET UP EACH BUSINESS AREA—TECH SUPPORT, SALES, HR, OFFICE SERVICES, MARKETING—AND GAVE EACH ITS OWN BOARD OF ADVISORS. EACH AREA IS RESPONSIBLE FOR ITS OWN PLAN AND FOR MEET-ING QUARTERLY TO MEASURE AND REPORT ON PROGRESS. IT'S BEEN VERY EFFECTIVE FOR US.

# YOUR ROLES AND KEY RESPONSIBILITIES

IT AMAZES ME HOW DIFFERENT COMPANIES CONSISTENTLY EXPERIENCE THE SAME THINGS WHEN THEY GROW. I WISH SOMEONE HAD LAID OUT FOR ME A LONG TIME AGO THE DIFFERENT STAGES OF GROWTH. IT WOULD HAVE MADE MY JOB MUCH, MUCH EASIER. AS IT TURNED OUT, IT WASN'T OBVIOUS TO ME WHAT WAS HAPPENING UNTIL WE GOT TO ABOUT 250 EMPLOYEES; BUT WHEN WE DID, THE MANAGEMENT TEAM AND I BECAME VERY PROACTIVE. WE KNEW THIS THING WAS GOING TO BREAK, AND WE FIGURED OUT WHAT IT WAS GOING TO LOOK LIKE AND WHY IT WAS HAPPENING. SO WHEN WE FIRST SAW SOME SIGNS OF DETERIORATION IN THE COMPANY, WE REACTED RIGHT AWAY AND CHANGED EVERYTHING. WE COMPLETELY RESTRUCTURED MANAGEMENT. IT WORKED LIKE A CHARM, AND THE SURPRISING THING WAS HOW LITTLE DISRUPTION IT CAUSED TO DO THE RIGHT THING, HOW FEW PEOPLE IN THE COMPANY EVEN NOTICED HOW MUCH WE CHANGED.

Moving into Continuous Growth means your roles and responsibilities must undergo some major changes. You, the leader, will need to move out of operations and focus on issues outside the company. Your top team will need to be responsible for managing the company, as well as alignment and integration. They have to work together and work cross-functionally. There will be times when you will need to move back into the organization to be a catalyst for change, the chief of culture, and to strengthen or rebuild the organization.

All this will require you to creatively apply all of your original entrepreneurial strengths as well as all of your new leadership skills as you move into these four new roles:

- Change Catalyst
- Organization Builder
- Strategic Innovator
- Chief of Culture

You are the only one who can fulfill these four critical roles. The company's survival and growth depend on your ability to handle these responsibilities effectively (see the following figure).

THE ORGANIZATION MUST CHANGE. IF THERE'S EXTERNAL CHANGE, IF THE ENVIRONMENT IS CHANGING, THE ORGANIZATION MUST CHANGE AS WELL. THIS IS WHAT I MISSED IN THE IPO. WE TOOK THE COMPANY PUBLIC, AND IT TOOK US TOO LONG TO REALIZE THAT WE NEEDED A DIFFERENT ORGANIZATION TO TAKE ADVANTAGE OF THE NEW OPPORTUNITIES. THAT'S, FOR ME, STILL A VERY PAINFUL LESSON. SO WHEN I SAY THE ORGANIZATION MUST CHANGE, IT'S REALLY THE PEOPLE WHO MUST CHANGE. WHEN WE WERE IN TURBULENT WATER, WHEN THINGS WERE NOT SO GOOD, I STRUGGLED TO KEEP SOME OF THE PEOPLE WHO'D BEEN WITH US A LONG TIME. I FELT LOYALTY TO THEM, AND I KNEW THE VALUE THEY CONTRIBUTED. BUT THE TRUTH WAS, THEIR HEART WASN'T IN IT ANYMORE. I WOULD HAVE BEEN BETTER OFF JETTISONING SOME OF THEM, LETTING THEM GO IF THEIR HEART WASN'T IN IT. I NEEDED A GROUP OF COMMITTED EMPLOYEES AT THAT POINT IN TIME.

AND NEW PEOPLE COME IN ENERGIZED. BUT SOMETIMES IT'S NOT JUST CHANGING PEOPLE, IT'S CHANGING THE STRUCTURE, BECAUSE THE ORGANIZATION HAS TO FUNCTION DIFFERENTLY. AND THIS IS THE TIME WHEN OUTSIDERS ADD MORE VALUE THAN ANY OTHER. WHETHER IT'S OUTSIDERS WHO HELP YOU WITH YOUR LAYOFF OR CONSULTANTS WHO HELP YOU DEFINE A VISION, I FOUND THAT OUTSIDERS ADDED A LOT OF CREDIBILITY AT A TIME WHEN PEOPLE QUESTIONED MANAGEMENT.

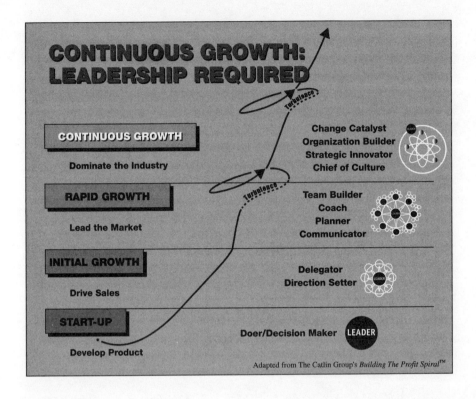

CONTINUOUS GROWTH:
LEADERSHIP REQUIRED

**CONTINUOUS GROWTH**

Dominate the Industry

Change Catalyst
Organization Builder
Strategic Innovator
Chief of Culture

**RAPID GROWTH**

Lead the Market

Team Builder
Coach
Planner
Communicator

**INITIAL GROWTH**

Drive Sales

Delegator
Direction Setter

**START-UP**

Develop Product

Doer/Decision Maker    LEADER

Adapted from The Catlin Group's *Building The Profit Spiral*™

## CHANGE CATALYST

Change Catalyst is the first new role you assume as you transform from a leader of Rapid Growth to a leader of Continuous Growth. This is a critical role and one that you will maintain as you move your company through cycle after cycle of reinvention. The simple fact is that the company must make significant changes to completely fulfill its growth potential. If this planning and transforming isn't done effectively, the company will start spinning its wheels, lose focus on the big picture, move back to reactive crisis mode, lose money, and/or decline significantly. It's at this point that many entrepreneurs say they "hit the wall." Some leave, others are asked to move aside or move out of the company entirely because they don't seem able to take the company to the next level of growth fast enough. It is so common for savvy start-up entrepreneurs to stumble at this stage of company growth that many venture capitalists routinely replace the leader as a condition of investing. Once there's the slightest question about the entrepreneur's leadership abilities, boards and investors seek a replacement very quickly.

WITH OUR NEW FUNDING, WE COULD HAVE DONE A LOT OF ACQUISITIONS. AND THE PROBLEM WAS, OUR ORGANIZATION WAS NOT STRUCTURED TO DO ACQUISITIONS. WE HAD BUILT OUR PRODUCTS INTERNALLY. WE HAD A TEAM THAT WORKED ON A CONSENSUS BASIS. WHEN YOU TAKE THAT APPROACH, IN THIS NEW ARENA, NOTHING HAPPENS. WE KEPT LOOKING AT ACQUISITIONS. I KEPT ENCOURAGING IT. WE'D LOOK AT THINGS, AND SOMEBODY WOULD FIND A REASON NOT TO DO IT.

AND OVER THE COURSE OF ABOUT 18 MONTHS WHILE OUR STOCK SOARED, WE DID NO ACQUISITIONS. BY THE TIME WE DID OUR FIRST ACQUISITION, IT WAS TWO MONTHS AFTER WE HIT THE WALL, AND OUR STOCK PRICE HAD DECLINED BY ABOUT 40 PERCENT. SO THAT ACQUISITION COST US FAR MORE THAN IT NEEDED TO. AND IT COULD AND SHOULD HAVE BEEN DONE MUCH, MUCH SOONER. BUT THAT REQUIRED AN ORGANIZATIONAL CHANGE. I SHOULD HAVE RECOGNIZED EARLIER THAT WE NEEDED TO RESTRUCTURE OUR ORGANIZATION TO TAKE ADVANTAGE OF NEW OPPORTUNITIES.

I SHOULD HAVE IMMEDIATELY BROUGHT IN A VICE PRESIDENT FOR BUSINESS DEVELOPMENT. I DON'T THINK ANYBODY IN MY ORGANIZATION WAS RIGHT FOR THAT ROLE. BUT I SHOULD HAVE CREATED THAT NEW ROLE, SO THAT WE HAD SOMEONE WHO OWNED THE RESPONSIBILITY, AND THE REST OF THE ORGANIZATION GOT A MESSAGE, "WE ARE GOING TO DO THIS." THEY DIDN'T GET THAT MESSAGE. THEY JUST GOT THE MESSAGE THAT IT MIGHT BE INTERESTING. I WASN'T STRONG ENOUGH.

You don't need to let this situation happen to you. Use your considerable entrepreneurial talent, along with your new skills of collaborative teamwork, planning, and communication, to establish yourself in the role of Change Catalyst. Inspire people to work proactively with you to identify the issues and meet the significant challenges of growth. This role is vital as the company enters Continuous Growth. It will also be critical in the future as the business approaches other inevitable turning points that will require fundamental reexamination and reinvention of how the company operates. You will have to make changes again and again to meet the requirements of ever-higher levels of success.

WHEN WE MADE OUR FIRST BIG ACQUISITION, I TOLD PEOPLE THINGS WEREN'T GOING TO CHANGE. I WAS DEAD WRONG. VERY QUICKLY, OUR COMPANY SHIFTED FROM BEING TRANSACTION-BASED TO ONE THAT HAS TRANSACTIONS AS WELL AS SOFTWARE AND CONSULTING SERVICES. IT CAUGHT ME BY SURPRISE AND I NEEDED TO ADD SOME FOLKS PRETTY QUICKLY. SO INSTEAD OF NO CHANGES, I FOUND WE HAD THE KIND OF CHANGES THAT ARE HUGE, LIKE TECTONIC PLATES SHIFTING UNDER OUR FEET.

THE QUESTIONS OUR EXECUTIVE TEAM DEALS WITH NOW ARE TYPICALLY LARGER, ENTERPRISE-WIDE, LONGER-TERM KINDS OF ISSUES. THE BEST USE OF OUR TIME IS TO CREATE THE BIG-PICTURE PLANS AND GOALS, SET DIRECTIONS, AND DECIDE HOW TO DEAL WITH SWEEPING CHANGES AND "GLOBAL" ISSUES IN OUR WORLD. THEN OUR JOB IS TO TAKE THOSE BIGGER ISSUES AND CREATE BITE-SIZED PACKAGES THAT CAN BE COMMUNICATED TO THE REST OF THE ORGANIZATION IN CONSISTENT WAYS. WE LEARNED THIS THE HARD WAY WHEN WE MADE A BIG DECISION, THEN SENT THE MESSAGE OUT TO THE ORGANIZA-TION IN BASKIN-ROBBINS' 31-VARIETIES WAYS. IT CREATED MORE CONFUSION THAN ANYTHING. NOW WE MAKE SURE THAT THE EXECUTIVE TEAM NOT ONLY MAKES BIG-PICTURE DECISIONS, BUT ALSO TRANSLATES THEM IN CONSISTENT WAYS SO THEY CAN BE COMMUNICATED TO THE REST OF THE STAFF IN SMALLER, ACTIONABLE ITEMS.

Your Continuous Growth plan should include the same major components as the plan you implemented during Rapid Growth. However, you will have new definitions of market and customer focus, mission, vision and objectives, strategies and tactics, organizational structure and processes, and innovative culture (see "Building the Profit Spiral™" in Chapter 3). The planning process must be one that does the following:

- Is open and participatory

- Pushes for strategic and out-of-the-box thinking

- Encourages your entire management team and all functional areas to review their current ways of operating; challenge all assumptions; and create new, innovative methods to achieve the new growth

Remember that planning is not an event but a continual process (see the following figure). In order to navigate turbulence and generate the energy needed to move up the Continuous Growth curve, make sure everyone in the company has learned the funda-mentals of planning in a growth company:

- **Discovery**—Constantly gather feedback and input on the external and internal environment, routinely challenge assumptions, and continually reassess to make sure that the company's plans are aligned with what the market needs.

- **Visioning and Planning**—Create new plans and initiatives that synthesize the new feedback and fit with your picture of the company's potential for new growth.

- **Action and Results**—Execute the new plans, measure progress, and make new discoveries that lead back to the "Discovery" part of the planning loop.

- **Communication**—Communicate clearly and completely all along the way.

If you use this planning process, you and your executive team can manage Continuous Growth wisely and effectively.

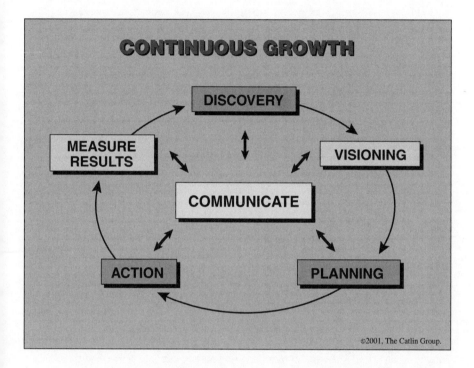

THE MORE THE ORGANIZATION IS CHANGING, THE MORE COMMUNICATION YOU NEED, AND WITH ALL OF YOUR CONSTITUENCIES. YOU'VE GOT TO COMMUNICATE WITH YOUR BOARD, EVEN WHEN—ESPECIALLY WHEN—THINGS AREN'T GOING WELL. WHEN THE BOARD ISN'T HAPPY, IT'S LESS PLEASANT, BUT THAT'S WHEN YOU NEED TO COMMUNICATE MORE THAN EVER. YOU'VE GOT TO FIGHT THAT INSTINCT TO AVOID IT. AND YOU'VE GOT TO GIVE YOUR MANAGEMENT TEAM THE REINFORCEMENT IT NEEDS TO COMMUNICATE, TOO. CONTINUALLY ASK EACH OF YOUR CONSTITUENCIES WHAT KIND OF COMMUNICATION IS NEEDED. ASK YOURSELF THE SAME QUESTION. IT'S ABSOLUTELY ESSENTIAL AT EVERY LEVEL.

As the leader, you may be the only one who sees the need for the transformation. You must lead the reinvention process, and you must make sure that your management team is aligned with it. Other people may not think such fundamental change is necessary. They may try to persuade you to get by with tweaking the original plan, doing minor reorganization, hiring a few new people, changing compensation structures, or doing some training. But these approaches will be only temporary fixes; transformation is the only real solution.

IT'S MY JOB TO GET THE TEAM WORKING CREATIVELY ON A STRATEGIC ISSUE OR A TOUGH OPERATING PROBLEM OR A PERSONNEL PROBLEM THAT'S REALLY IMPORTANT TO THE COMPANY. A BIG PART OF MY RESPONSIBILITY IS TO QUESTION EVERYTHING AND ANYTHING. NOTHING IS REALLY SACRED. WE CERTAINLY HAVE OUR CORE VALUES, BUT EVEN THOSE HAVE TO BE REVISITED AND REFRESHED.

ONE OF THE THINGS THAT WE DO IN OUR DISCUSSIONS IS TO TAKE SOME OF THE THINGS THAT ARE REALLY FUNDAMENTAL TO OUR BUSINESS—LARGE REVENUE GENERATORS, MAJOR CLIENTS, THAT KIND OF THING—AND TALK ABOUT WHAT IF THE WORLD ISN'T LIKE THAT?

WHAT IF THAT CLIENT GOES AWAY? OR WHAT IF OUR CUSTOMERS DON'T WORRY ANYMORE ABOUT THE PROBLEMS WE CAN SOLVE? GET AT THE FUNDAMENTALS OF YOUR BUSINESS AND THINK ABOUT HOW YOU'D DEAL WITH THAT ENVIRONMENT. ARE YOU GOING TO JUST CLOSE UP SHOP? OF COURSE NOT. YOU'RE GOING TO HAVE TO DO SOMETHING ELSE. AND TRY TO IMAGINE THAT AHEAD OF TIME. THAT REALLY GETS THE CREATIVE JUICES GOING.

USING TEAMS AS MECHANISMS FOR GETTING TO NEW SOLUTIONS IS IMPORTANT. NOTHING LIKE HAVING SOME FOLKS FROM THE SERVICE DELIVERY GROUP AND THE MARKETING GROUP WORKING WITH SOME OF THE FOLKS FROM ENGINEERING ON AN ENGINEERING-RELATED ISSUE TO GET SOME DIFFERENT PERSPECTIVES AND DIFFERENT IDEAS. THAT'S HOW WE DISCOVER EXCITING NEW OPPORTUNITIES.

There will always be people who choose not to make the journey. Even though you built a strong team in Rapid Growth, all members may not be capable of making the changes required to take the company to the next level, of making the leap being demanded of them. Part of your Change Catalyst role is to be constantly asking, "Can this management team take us to a whole new level?" Be proactive and work to be sure you have the right team in place.

THERE WAS A POINT WHEN WE WERE IN THE MIDDLE OF A HUGE TRANSITION, A MAJOR CHANGE THAT INVOLVED MOVING OUR PRODUCT TO THE INTERNET. THE VICE PRESIDENT OF SALES REALLY FAILED TO ENGAGE WITH THE NEW PLAN. HE SAID HE DIDN'T HAVE TIME TO HELP BECAUSE HE HAD TO BRING IN SALES. SO HE DIDN'T DO WHAT HE WAS EXPECTED TO DO IN THE STRATEGIC PLANNING PROCESS. WHAT THAT DID WAS SIGNAL TO EVERYBODY THAT HE WAS NOT RIGHT FOR THE COMPANY. HE WAS RESISTANT TO THIS IMPORTANT CHANGE. AND NOW HE'S OUT. HE JUST WASN'T GOING TO MAKE IT IN THE NEW COMPANY.

There are ways to help people with the transformation. Explain why you're making the change. Share the market data and customer information. Be honest with people and get their input. If you communicate the reasoning behind change and the plan for making it happen, people will find it easier to get behind the new dynamics of the company.

> IF I HAD IT TO DO OVER AGAIN, I WOULD TALK MORE ABOUT WHY WE NEEDED TO CHANGE. I WOULD DO MORE RETRAINING OF PEOPLE AND GIVE THEM A CHANCE TO LEARN NEW SKILLS. BUT IN THAT TURBULENT CYCLE, THINGS WERE MOVING FAST AND WE DIDN'T TAKE THE TIME TO DO THIS AS WELL AS WE COULD HAVE. I DON'T THINK EVERYONE WOULD HAVE STAYED. BUT I THINK A FEW MORE MIGHT HAVE MADE IT.

# ORGANIZATION BUILDER

As Organization Builder, you must focus on setting up the organization so it can support Continuous Growth in scale, scope, and complexity. This requires two key changes in the way you previously worked, both dealing with team building: You must build the executive team to become leaders of growth, and you must establish a network of teams for bottom-up planning and operations.

## BUILDING THE EXECUTIVE TEAM TO BECOME LEADERS OF GROWTH

You cannot achieve Continuous Growth if you try to do all the leadership tasks yourself. Sharing your leadership tasks with your managers extends the CEO's role to include the whole team and dramatically increases the company's capacity to grow. It's not unlike the changes you made during Initial Growth, when you first began handing off decision-making responsibilities. But how do you do this?

First, you empower your executive team to run the company day-to-day, while you stay completely out of operations and instead focus on the strategic functions required as CEO. This often means designating someone to be COO and/or reorganizing the executive team's roles, while redefining your own role as the strategic, not operational, leader of the company. Some entrepreneurs have even rented an off-site office where they go several times a week to do their thinking and planning. Let your team become true corporate leaders in their own right. That's what will free you to focus on strategic management.

> I USED TO HAVE MY HAND IN EVERY BIG DECISION, BUT THAT WAS WHEN WE WERE MUCH SMALLER. NOW I HAVE A PARTNER WHO IS IN CHARGE OF OUR OPERATIONS WHILE I HANDLE STRATEGY AND LONG-TERM PLANNING. IT'S HARD FOR ME. HE DOESN'T DO SOME THINGS THE WAY I WOULD DO THEM. BUT

I TOTALLY TRUST THE GUY. I KNOW HE CAN HANDLE ANYTHING OPERATIONAL. AND I KNOW MY ROLE IS CRITICAL TO OUR FUTURE. I'M THE ONE IN TOUCH WITH OUR INDUSTRY, WATCHING OUR COMPETITORS, AND MAKING THE DECISIONS THAT WILL AFFECT WHAT WE DO IN THE YEARS TO COME.

Second, recognize that your reach as strategic leader can extend only so far. You have to transfer leadership to your managers and develop an effective executive team whose members operate as "Leaders of Growth." Start by creating a job description that is different from the description of each member's functional job as vice president of a department. Create a job description that is explicitly for leaders of the company. Six areas of responsibility should be included in the Executive Team Job Description (see box).

Third, be explicit in defining your expectations of each member of the management team. You will need to clearly communicate which tasks you will continue to do and which ones truly belong to others. They must understand and accept the fact that each of them wears two hats. They must handle both their operational roles as leaders of their functional areas and their strategic roles as leaders of the company. The functional roles are easy to define, since that's what they do every day, but the strategic leadership role is more difficult to pin down and needs to be clearly articulated by you.

EVEN THOUGH I WORKED WITH MY EXECUTIVE TEAM MEMBERS ON OUR STRATEGIC PLAN AND I THOUGHT THEY WERE CARRYING OUT THEIR DUTIES AS LEADERS, I BEGAN TO HEAR FROM MIDDLE MANAGERS THAT THE SENIOR TEAM WAS MICROMANAGING THEM AND THAT THEY DID NOT FEEL EMPOWERED. THAT MEANT MY EXECUTIVES WERE STILL TOO ORIENTED TO THE SHORT TERM, TOO HANDS-ON OPERATIONALLY, AND WEREN'T DEVELOPING OTHER LEADERS. WE HAD JUST GONE THROUGH THE IPO AND OUR BOARD CHAIRMAN SAT ME DOWN AND POINTED OUT THAT I HAD A MANAGEMENT TEAM THAT JUST WASN'T STRONG ENOUGH TO TAKE THE COMPANY TO THE NEXT LEVEL. THAT WAS WHEN I HAD TO EXERT MORE INFLUENCE AND TELL THEM I EXPECTED THEM TO BE LONGER-TERM, BIGGER-PICTURE STRATEGIC THINKERS AND CREATORS OF AN EMPOWERING CULTURE. WE HAD TO DEVELOP A NEW WAY OF FUNCTIONING AS A TEAM SO WE COULD BE SURE WE WERE FOCUSING ON THE BIGGER ISSUES AND BECOMING COACHES FOR THE NEXT-LEVEL MANAGERS. IT WAS A VERY DIFFICULT TRANSITION FOR THEM—LIKE PULLING TEETH SINCE THEY WERE SO CAUGHT UP IN THE FAST PACE OF THE DAY-TO-DAY.

# VITAL SIGNS: BUILDING THE EXECUTIVE TEAM AS LEADERS OF GROWTH™

**Responsibilities of the Executive Team**

**Leading growth.** Effective Executive Teams paint the big picture and create a plan that produces all the requirements for growth. The plan must cover the following areas of company operations:

- Market and customer focus
- Mission and values
- Vision and objectives
- Strategies and plans
- Structure and processes
- Innovative culture

The Executive Team then uses this plan to focus and drive every team and individual objectives throughout the company.

**Leading for alignment.** Effective Executive Teams create clarity and alignment throughout the entire organization with frequent, consistent, and systematic communication and involvement of staff. As a result, everyone in the company is on the same page.

**Leading the culture.** Effective Executive Teams define and evangelize the innovative culture required for growth. They work together to model and support that culture.

**Attracting and retaining awesome people.** Awesome people are self-motivated; share the company's values; are respectful, creative, perpetual learners; and enable everyone around them to do a better job than they could do on their own. The Effective Executive Team must understand that they are accountable for following agreed-upon processes for hiring, retaining, and rewarding highly talented people who will drive the company's growth.

**Managing team pitfalls.** Effective Executive Teams manage the pitfalls common to all teams as well as the pitfalls that are unique to their own team dynamics. They learn to use processes for balanced decision making, creative problem solving, giving feedback, learning from successes and failures, and healthy conflict resolution.

*cont...*

*-continued*

 **Learning from each other.** Effective Executive Teams understand and value each other's differences, priorities, and styles. They leverage their differences, seek feedback on their own effectiveness, continually learn from each other, and help each other be successful.

© *2001, The Catlin Group. Building the Executive Team as Leaders of Growth is a trademark of Katherine Catlin.*

As strategic company leaders, each member of the team must work with you on these aspects of leadership:

- Creating a strategic plan for growth
- Setting the company's direction and communicating consistent messages to gain alignment
- Hiring and retaining awesome people
- Building a culture and organization that support continual growth
- Making sure the team's work is a role model for all teams
- Learning from each other and fully leveraging their different skills

The following box, "How Does Your Team Rate?" provides a quick way to assess your team's performance—and your own.

THE CEO'S ROLE, WITH HELP FROM THE EXECUTIVE TEAM, IS TO ESTABLISH DIRECTION, VISION, AND FOCUS. THEY ALSO NEED TO DEVELOP FINANCIAL STRATEGIES (THAT IS, HOW WE'LL MAKE MONEY AND HOW WE'LL SPEND IT) AND WITH CONSCIOUS CULTURE-BUILDING STRATEGIES (THAT IS, HOW WE'LL OPERATE AND DEVELOP AS AN ORGANIZATION); IN ADDITION, THEY MUST SET GOALS WITH TARGETED RESULTS; HUGE, SEEMINGLY IMPOSSIBLE ONES SO PEOPLE KNOW THEY CAN'T STAY "IN THE BOX" TO ACCOMPLISH THEM. THEN THEY NEED TO STAY FOCUSED AND MONITOR PROGRESS TOWARD THE TARGETS AND MAKE SURE COMMUNICATIONS COMING FROM THE MANAGEMENT TEAM ARE CONSISTENT AND ALIGNED. IT'S CRITICAL THAT NO ONE SHOWS ONE CRACK OF DISAGREEMENT OUTSIDE THE TEAM WHILE THEY ARE BUILDING CONSENSUS AND BUY-IN THROUGHOUT THE COMPANY.

## VITAL SIGNS: HOW DOES YOUR TEAM RATE?

You might want to rate your team, as well as yourself, on each of the six responsibilities for Effective Executive Teams. Be honest and then share your assessment with your team members.

On a scale of 1 (low) to 5 (high), how do you rate each team member on these leadership roles:

- Leading growth
- Leading for alignment
- Leading the culture
- Attracting and retaining awesome people
- Managing team pitfalls
- Learning from each other

How do you rate yourself?

THE CEO MUST MAKE A SMALL NUMBER OF KEY DECISIONS ON HIS/HER OWN, WITH APPROPRIATE INPUT FROM OTHERS, AND THEN MAKE SURE THEY'RE COMMUNICATED CROSS-FUNCTIONALLY. ALSO, I PAY ATTENTION TO BUILDING THE CULTURE. YOU CAN'T FAKE IT WITH LIP SERVICE. YOU *MUST* HAVE CREDIBILITY BY DRAWING THE LINE OF WHAT YOU WILL AND WON'T TOLERATE—AND STICK TO IT. INSIDE THE EXECUTIVE TEAM, I WANT TO HAVE EVERYONE BRING A UNIQUE PERSPECTIVE, BIASED BY HIS OR HER FUNCTIONAL EXPERTISE. THEY NEED TO FIGHT FOR WHAT THEY REALLY BELIEVE IN, UNDERSTAND EACH OTHER, AND HELP FIND THE BEST SOLUTIONS—AND THEN BUY IN TO THE FINAL DECISION, EVEN WHEN IT MIGHT NOT AGREE WITH THEIR ORIGINAL POSITION.

MANAGING THE TEAM IS ONE OF THE MOST DIFFICULT PARTS OF THE JOB. IF YOU HAVE BROUGHT TOGETHER A GOOD TEAM, YOU HAVE PEOPLE WHO HAVE

EGOS AND STRONG POINTS OF VIEW. THEY HAVE GREAT EXPERIENCE, IF YOU HIRED A+ PLAYERS. THEY WANT TO CONTRIBUTE. THEY HAVE A HUNGER TO CONTRIBUTE. THEY MAY EVEN HAVE A HUNGER TO LEAD, WHICH I THINK IS A GREAT THING, BECAUSE YOU SHOULD HAVE A "LEADERFUL" ORGANIZATION.

HOW DO WE DO IT? WE HAVE OFF-SITE MEETINGS A COUPLE OF TIMES A YEAR, WHERE WE GO AWAY FOR SEVERAL DAYS. WE HAVE ASSIGNMENTS FOR THOSE MEETINGS. YOU DON'T GET TO JUST COME AND PUT YOUR FEET UP. YOU HAVE HOMEWORK ASSIGNMENTS. YOU HAVE TO COME PREPARED, WHICH REALLY FORCES CRITICAL THINKING ON STRATEGIC ISSUES FOR THE COMPANY. WE THEN HAVE CROSS-FUNCTIONAL ASSIGNMENTS THAT COME OUT OF THOSE STRATEGIC MEETINGS. SO IF THERE'S AN INITIATIVE, FOR EXAMPLE, ON AN INTERNATIONAL AREA, THERE WILL BE A CROSS-FUNCTIONAL TEAM THAT WILL BE WORKING ON THAT INITIATIVE WITH A PROJECT PLAN AND MILESTONES AND REPORTS BACK TO THE ORGANIZATION, THE EXECUTIVE TEAM, AND THE REST OF THE ORGANIZATION ON THAT.

## ESTABLISHING A NETWORK OF TEAMS FOR BOTTOM-UP PLANNING AND OPERATIONS

With a larger number of employees, the executive team can no longer know everything about all activities in all parts of the company. As the Organization Builder, you need to set up a more "bottom-up" structure for planning and operations, using self-managed teams. This new organizational design keeps the decisions about overall vision and major corporate strategies at the executive team level. Yet it does not require the executive team to make all the decisions about operations, since they don't know as much as their staff about what's really working at all levels. The charter of the self-managed teams is to participate in the continuous Discovery-Visioning-Planning-Action-Results loop in their own areas of responsibility. Thus, knowledge from throughout the organization is included in the company's overall planning and implementation process.

I AM AN ADVOCATE OF A BOTTOM-UP PARTICIPATIVE APPROACH BECAUSE THAT'S WHERE THE IDEAS COME FROM. VERY FEW OF THE IDEAS WE HAVE THESE DAYS ARE MINE. MY JOB IS NOT TO COME UP WITH ALL THE NEW IDEAS, BUT TO FIND THE GOOD ONES, TO MAKE SURE THEY ARE ENCOURAGED, AND TO MAKE SURE THEY GET DONE. YOU'VE GOT TO HAVE THE BOTTOM-UP SYSTEM FOR THAT. IT MAKES EVERYONE FEEL THAT THEY CAN EXHIBIT PERSONAL LEADERSHIP, THAT LEADING THE COMPANY IS THEIR JOB, TOO.

I HAVE A VERY STRONG BELIEF THAT YOU MUST HAVE TEAMS BECAUSE THAT'S THE ONLY WAY YOU'RE GOING TO GET TO USE ALL THE BRAIN CELLS IN YOUR ORGANIZATION. THAT'S REALLY THE ONLY THING YOU HAVE TO COMPETE WITH. OTHER PEOPLE HAVE THEIR BRAIN CELLS WORKING AGAINST YOU. AND I THINK THE ONLY WAY REALLY TO DO THAT IS IN A TEAM KIND OF ENVIRONMENT WHERE YOU INVITE, ENCOURAGE, AND INVIGORATE ALL THOSE BRAIN CELLS TO WORK ON THE ISSUES. I THINK IT GIVES YOU THE KIND OF BROAD PERSPECTIVE THAT YOU HAVE TO HAVE IN YOUR BUSINESS.

ALSO, I THINK THAT TEAMS GIVE YOU BUILT-IN BACKUP AND REDUNDANCY. IF YOU'VE GOT ONLY ONE PERSON DOING THINGS, AND THAT PERSON FALLS OFF A CLIFF OR GETS HIT BY A TRUCK, YOU'VE PROBABLY LOST QUITE A BIT. IF YOU HAVE TEAMS WORKING ON THINGS, THEN YOU CAN HAVE THE COMINGS AND GOINGS OF INDIVIDUALS IN THAT TEAM AND STILL CONTINUE THE FORWARD MOMENTUM OF THE PROJECT OR THE STRATEGIC INITIATIVE FOR THE COMPANY OVERALL. I THINK IT'S IMPORTANT TO BE ABLE TO HAVE THAT. I THINK WHEN IT WORKS WELL, IT IS THE MOST CREATIVE, INVIGORATING, HONEST REVENUE- AND PROFIT-PRODUCING MODE THAT YOU CAN HAVE IN A COMPANY. AND WHEN IT DOESN'T WORK WELL, IT CAN TEAR YOU APART AND CAUSE YOU TO CRASH AND BURN PRETTY QUICKLY.

BUT HAVING SAID ALL THOSE GREAT THINGS ABOUT TEAMS, I THINK TEAMING IS AN UNNATURAL ACT. IT'S EASY TO TALK ABOUT, BUT THINK ABOUT WHAT BEING IN A TEAM REALLY REQUIRES. IT DOESN'T MEAN THAT YOU ALL HOLD HANDS AND SMILE AT EACH OTHER ALL THE TIME. IT MEANS THAT THERE IS AN ABILITY TO DEBATE, TO ARGUE, TO GET VERY ENERGIZED AROUND AN ISSUE, TO COME TO RESOLUTION ON THAT ISSUE, AND KNOW THAT THERE'S NO HIDDEN AGENDA UNDER THE TABLE, THAT YOU'RE REALLY TRYING TO GET TO THE SAME PLACE, EVEN THOUGH YOU'RE COMING FROM VERY DIFFERENT PERSPECTIVES. AND YOU CAN HAVE VERY HEATED DISCUSSIONS. AND THAT'S OKAY. IN FACT, IT'S GREAT. IT'S A FINE THING TO DO.

TO HAVE ALL OF THAT DYNAMIC, THAT'S GREAT, BUT THEN YOU HAVE TO HAVE PERFORMANCE. WHAT DID YOU SET OUT TO DO? HAVE YOU DONE IT, ON TIME, AT THE LEVEL YOU SAID YOU WERE GOING TO? HAVE YOU MET YOUR COMMITMENTS TO YOUR CLIENTS, YOUR SHAREHOLDERS, AND EACH OTHER? SO THERE'S A LOT OF WORK GOING ON IN THOSE TEAMS. AND FOR A LOT OF PEOPLE THAT IS REALLY UNCOMFORTABLE. EVERYONE LIKES TO TALK ABOUT WORKING IN TEAMS, BUT A LOT OF PEOPLE ARE NOT COMFORTABLE FUNCTIONING OR OPERATING AS PART OF A TEAM.

As strategic responsibility is pushed to all parts of the company, the teams must:

- Develop and execute plans in alignment with the companywide vision and strategy.

- Continuously improve upon results, evaluate performance, and reward or redirect people's efforts as needed.

- Work across functions to achieve those results efficiently.

- Use creative thinking and problem solving to meet the challenges imposed by growth.

- Experiment with initiatives that win more customers; build better products; offer novel services; institute faster, and smarter, better methods to keep the company in Continuous Growth mode as a market winner.

BASED ON VERY CLEAR MARKET SIGNALS AND CUSTOMER FEEDBACK, I HAD TO TAKE THE COMPANY THROUGH A TRANSITION TO DEVELOP A WHOLE NEW PRODUCT LINE. WE DIDN'T WANT TO ELIMINATE OUR PREVIOUS BUSINESS ENTIRELY. IT WAS STILL PROFITABLE, STILL PAYING THE BILLS, AND WE WANTED TO PRESERVE SOME OF IT. WE ALSO HAD SOME CUSTOMERS WE WANTED TO BRING ACROSS AND SOME VALUABLE INTELLECTUAL PROPERTY THAT WE WANTED TO USE. BUT WE NEEDED TO GET AWAY FROM THE OLD MINDSET AND CULTURE. SOME EMPLOYEES WERE VERY COMFORTABLE WITH THE OLD WAYS, BUT I WANTED TO POUR 10 FEET OF CONCRETE AND START OVER. THAT WAS QUITE A SET OF CHALLENGES.

SO WE CREATED A NEW DEVELOPMENT TEAM WITH SOME PEOPLE I THOUGHT WERE ENTREPRENEURIAL AND FRESH-THINKING. WE TOOK AWAY THEIR RESPONSIBILITIES IN THE EXISTING BUSINESS AND GAVE THEM A LOT OF ROOM IN UNCHARTED TERRITORY. THEY GOT TO HIRE SOME NEW PEOPLE, WHICH I THINK HELPED A LOT. THEY BUILT A BETTER PRODUCT A LOT FASTER THAN THEY WOULD HAVE IF THEY HAD STAYED WITHIN THE OLD STRUCTURE. IN FACT, IT MIGHT NEVER HAVE BEEN BUILT.

This bottom-up design demands excellent management and communication skills and processes, so that information about plans, goals, measurements, and progress is known and understood throughout the organization. You and your executive team must consciously nurture and create this required alignment.

RIGHT NOW, OUR EXECUTIVE TEAM MEETS EVERY WEEK. I'VE ADDED QUITE A FEW PEOPLE TO THAT TEAM, AND THOSE MEETINGS ARE AN IMPORTANT WAY FOR US TO LEARN ABOUT EACH OTHER. WHAT DO WE DO AT THOSE MEETINGS? WE REPORT ON STRATEGIC INITIATIVES AND OUR PROGRESS WITH THEM. WE TALK ABOUT EVENTS WE EXPECT IN THE UPCOMING WEEK THAT HAVE CROSS-FUNCTIONAL IMPACT SO THAT THESE FOLKS CAN TELL THEIR TEAM LEADERS,

WHO CAN INFORM THEIR TEAMS IN A ONE-ON-ONE WAY INSTEAD OF IN AN E-MAIL THAT GOES OUT TO THE WHOLE COMPANY. WE REASSESS AND REALIGN OURSELVES. WHEN THINGS ARE GETTING OFF-TRACK, WE CAN PULL BACK INTO FOCUS. DOING THAT ON A WEEKLY BASIS REALLY HELPS US.

## STRATEGIC INNOVATOR

As Strategic Innovator, your role is to step out of and beyond the company to take an objective, expanded view of the external environment. You must constantly look for new trends and opportunities in the market and industry, as well as the most effective and innovative ways the company can help key customers grow and gain share in their markets.

You will spend much of your time away from the company, doing such things as attending targeted conferences where you speak as the expert "thought leader" to set direction for your industry and the market as a whole. You will also use these meetings to learn from other thought leaders about the latest developments and emerging trends. Your goals will be to act as the external spokesperson, gaining visibility for the company while simultaneously searching for the next big opportunity, the one that will lead to a new generation of change. This opportunity might be expanding product lines, discontinuing current products, adopting new technologies, or adding services or business units to capture new markets.

IN OUR FIRST COUPLE OF YEARS, I HAD NO TIME TO SPEND TRACKING CHANGES IN OUR INDUSTRY. IT TOOK EVERY MINUTE JUST TO PUT OUT FIRES AND KEEP US ON TRACK. IT GOT SO I FELT OUT OF TOUCH. WHEN I REALIZED THAT I HAD TO GET BACK OUT INTO THE WORLD TO GET THE PERSPECTIVE I NEEDED TO SET NEW STRATEGIC DIRECTIONS, I FOUND IT VERY HARD TO DO. I HAD TO LET CLIENTS WHO WERE USED TO GETTING ME ON THE PHONE KNOW THAT I WOULDN'T BE AVAILABLE AROUND THE CLOCK, THAT THEY HAD TO WORK WITH MY EMPLOYEES. IF THERE WAS A MAJOR PROBLEM, THEY COULD STILL COME TO ME, BUT I TOLD THEM, "I HIRED THIS PERSON TO HANDLE YOUR ACCOUNT BECAUSE I WANT YOU TO HAVE THE BEST SERVICE." IT WORKED. WE DIDN'T LOSE CUSTOMERS. AND I NEVER LOOKED BACK.

Being Strategic Innovator clearly taps your classic entrepreneurial strengths in seeking new possibilities for growth, especially in areas where others don't yet see the potential. It frees you to be creative and innovative by exposing you to more data, events, and people so you can create the next new vision—and keep the company on the cutting edge as a market and industry leader. Your executive team members need to help with some of the exploration. Establish regular strategic meetings to discuss what you are each learning about the opportunities for growth.

Once an opportunity is discovered and agreed upon as a new part of the company's strategy for growth, you may need to become its champion while your executives figure out how to incorporate the new initiative into their operational priorities. It is up to you to nurture the new initiative until someone on your team can own it and make it happen.

> YES, I WAS THE DRIVING FORCE BEHIND THE DEVELOPMENT OF THE DEAL THAT CREATED OUR STRATEGIC PARTNERSHIP BECAUSE I VIEWED IT AS A REAL STRATEGIC ACTIVITY FOR THE ORGANIZATION. IT DIDN'T FIT NICELY INTO ANYBODY ELSE'S ROLE IN THEIR OPERATING RESPONSIBILITIES. THAT IS NOT TO SAY THAT I DID IT ALONE, BECAUSE I NEVER COULD HAVE DONE THAT. THERE WAS LOTS AND LOTS OF PARTICIPATION ON THE PART OF OUR SALES ORGANIZATION, OUR MARKETING PEOPLE, AND OUR DEVELOPMENT PEOPLE. I TOOK IT ON AS A PERSONAL OBJECTIVE BECAUSE I THOUGHT IT WAS ABSOLUTELY CRITICAL TO THE SUCCESS OF OUR ORGANIZATION.

In this role, it is also important to find, develop, and carefully manage a variety of high-level partnerships and relationships that can be leveraged for growth. These may include joint ventures with other companies for product and/or market development, funding from outside investors or venture capitalists, new banking relationships, regular meetings with analysts, development of new channel partners, and alliances with other industry peers. The company can extend beyond its boundaries with these relationships and capitalize on new opportunities that would not be possible on its own. Finding appropriate partners will be one of the secrets of your company's success during Continuous Growth.

## CHIEF OF CULTURE

Chief of Culture is another role that only you can play. Your management team helps build and strengthen the culture, but you are the ultimate leader, the one who has the power to influence how people behave and operate to achieve the vision and goals of Continuous Growth. Being Chief of Culture combines all your other roles. The definition of the culture, values, and belief system is part of the planning process you lead as Change Catalyst. Your role as Organization Builder empowers the management team to be both strategic and operational leaders; and it enables the entire staff to work in teams, adding their input and staying aligned with the vision and plan. As Strategic Innovator, you are a role model for being close to the market, customers, and partners as sources of new ideas and possibilities for future growth.

> CULTURE HAS TO BE FELT, NOT JUST HEARD. IT CAN'T BE DELEGATED. IT REALLY IS THE CEO'S JOB.

Every company has a culture that either motivates or demotivates performance. You must shape your culture to support the pattern of development you want. Don't leave it to evolve on its own. The culture has been developing since you started the company. At each of the previous stages we've urged you to be proactive in building and modeling the culture. However, in Continuous Growth, the organization is too big for you to personally contact every person every day. Since you're playing more of an external role than ever before, it's critical that you be explicit about defining the culture you want, and that you provide positive and negative feedback regarding things that people do and say so as to institutionalize the elements of culture important to you. This is the only way to keep the company innovative and entrepreneurial as it grows and becomes a large organization.

The challenge is to stay entrepreneurial, maintaining the small-company feel and to avoid turning into the type of big company you've always hated.

> CULTURE COMES FROM VALUES. I HAPPEN TO HAVE PERSONAL VALUES. IT'S MY PREROGATIVE AS CEO TO NEVER WAIVER FROM MY SET OF VALUES. THEY CREATE OUR CULTURE, AND I'M FIRM WITH PEOPLE ABOUT IT. THIS IS IT. THIS IS OUR CULTURE. WE HAVE A ONE-WEEK ORIENTATION FOR ALL NEW EMPLOYEES TO LEARN ABOUT OUR COMPANY—AND I DON'T MEAN JUST ABOUT THEIR INDIVIDUAL JOBS. ONE FULL DAY IS SPENT ON CULTURE, VALUES, AND THE EXPECTATIONS INHERENT IN WORKING HERE. I JUST TOOK THE ENTIRE COMPANY TO DISNEY WORLD FOR THREE DAYS OF SERIOUS DISCUSSIONS ABOUT CULTURE AND VALUES AND HOW THEY MAP TO THE STRATEGIC OBJECTIVES OF THE COMPANY. IT COST $600,000, WHICH IS A LOT OF MONEY FOR A COMPANY OUR SIZE, BUT I'LL TELL YOU, I DIDN'T EVEN BREAK A SWEAT OVER IT. IT WAS WORTH EVERY CENT. I KNOW I'LL GET IT ALL BACK BIG-TIME! THE EMPLOYEES CAN GO OUT AND SAY, "OKAY, HE JUST PLOPPED DOWN 600 GRAND ON THIS. IT MUST BE IMPORTANT!" THAT'S A POWERFUL MESSAGE WITH LONG-LASTING EFFECTS.

The high-performance culture that stimulates continuous innovation and growth is characterized by results-focused, team-oriented, proactive problem-solvers who care about producing value for customers and who enjoy coming up with creative ideas to achieve the vision. To establish and maintain such a culture you need to do three things:

Institutionalize core values, create the Seven C's of Culture, and devise appropriate reward and recognition systems.

## INSTITUTIONALIZING CORE VALUES TO GUIDE EVERYONE'S BEHAVIOR

These core values must be based on your own internal beliefs about the right ways to operate to achieve success as a company. The process of defining and writing them is extremely useful, since it requires you and others to explore the real drivers of your own success. Once the values are in written form, they can be used as criteria for everyone to make decisions and prioritize tasks throughout the company. Then, everyone must be held accountable to these values—especially you!

Values are also essential in the hiring, orientation, training, and performance review processes. Your role is to demonstrate them in all your actions and activities, and to require your managers to deliver consistent messages, provide opportunities for everyone to learn about the values and understand what it means to "live by them." Being explicit about what you will and won't tolerate, and why, is one of the most powerful leadership tools you have for creating the culture of a great company.

WHEN WE WERE MUCH SMALLER, OUR CULTURE SPREAD BY OSMOSIS. EVERYBODY KNEW ME AND WHAT I VALUED AND WHAT I EXPECTED, AND I ASSUMED THEY UNDERSTOOD WHAT I WANTED THE COMPANY TO STAND FOR. THEN ONE DAY I LOOKED AROUND AND THERE WERE PEOPLE WORKING HERE THAT I HARDLY KNEW. HOW COULD THEY LEARN WHAT WAS EXPECTED? HOW COULD THEY SHARE MY VALUES IF I NEVER HAD TIME TO TALK TO THEM AS INDIVIDUALS? SO I WENT HOME ONE NIGHT AND SPENT THE EVENING WRITING DOWN THE VALUES I HAD AND THAT I WANTED THE COMPANY TO REFLECT. IT WAS THE FIRST TIME I HAD TRIED TO ARTICULATE MY VALUES SO CLEARLY, AND IT SURPRISED ME. THE LIST WASN'T LONG, BUT IT WAS SPECIFIC. EVERY EMPLOYEE KNOWS THESE VALUES—PROBABLY EVEN BETTER THAN THEY DID WHEN WE WERE SMALL—AND I AM MUCH MORE CONFIDENT THAT THE DECISIONS THEY MAKE ARE INFORMED BY THE VALUES I HOLD DEAR.

Every company must define the core values for itself. The values will be different, just as personalities are different in each company. One example of a set of values that supported successful growth was created by Ewing Marion Kauffman, founder of Marion Labs:

- Treat others as you want to be treated, with dignity, humility, and respect.

- Share the rewards with those who produce.

- Give back to the community that enabled your success.

That's it! They were simple, direct, yet specific enough to give direction and motivation to everyone who embraced them. These values were the foundation for all planning, all decisions, and all behavior as the company grew rapidly to a valuation of more than $6 billion when it merged with Merrell Dow in 1989. The values provided consistency of purpose and created an environment of trust, since everyone knew what he or she could expect from any other employee or manager. For example, Mr. Kauffman believed that "treating others as you want to be treated" meant that you were never late to meetings, that you provided information to people ahead of time so they could prepare, and that you ran efficient meetings that did not waste people's time.

These same three values were used to build the Kansas City Royals, the Kauffman Foundation, and the Kauffman Center for Entrepreneurial Leadership. The values became an important tool for Mr. Kauffman to create organizationwide alignment and enable everyone to make choices and decisions the way he would have made them. They also provided the rationale for explaining decisions to others. Members of the top management team and other associates, as he called them, were coached, were given warnings, and eventually fired if they did not adopt the behaviors that reflected the values Mr. Kauffman wanted to permeate his company.

Every entrepreneur must develop his or her own unique set of values. The key is specifically articulating the actions that visibly demonstrate the values and then communicating so everyone understands what they are.

OUR CULTURAL ENVIRONMENT WAS CREATED WHEN THE COMPANY FIRST STARTED. IT WAS BASED ON SOME REAL BASIC PRINCIPLES AND VALUES WE ALL AGREED ON:

(A) AUTONOMY. WE WANTED PEOPLE TO WORK INDEPENDENTLY AND WE WANTED TO TRUST THEM COMPLETELY TO DO THE WORK AND PRODUCE RESULTS.

(B) CONSENSUS/DEMOCRACY. WE FOUND THAT THE TEAM MADE THE BEST DECISIONS ABOUT HOW TO GET THINGS DONE. THIS WORKS WELL WITH STRONG LEADERSHIP.

(C) START-UP-DRIVEN ENERGY. WE WERE MONOMANIACAL IN OUR WORK HARD, WORK HARD, WORK, WORK, PLAY HARD ENVIRONMENT.

(D) REWARD FOR RESPONSIBILITY AND SELF-INITIATIVE. WE SENT A CRISP, CLEAR MESSAGE THAT IF YOU TAKE INITIATIVE, YOU GET A HIGH REWARD. IF NOT, IT'S A PROBLEM AND WE'LL HAVE TO TAKE ACTION. WE ALSO FOSTERED A SPIRIT OF PEOPLE OFFERING EACH OTHER HELP BY REACHING OUT PROACTIVELY TO SAY "WHAT CAN I DO TO HELP YOU?"

(E) LEARNING. THE MOST IMPORTANT PART OF EVERYONE'S JOB IS TO LEARN. WE HIRED AND GREW THE COMPANY WITH YOUNG, ENERGETIC, KNOWLEDGEABLE PEOPLE WHO WERE STILL "IMPRINTABLE" WITH CYCLES OF LEARNING, TEACHING OTHERS WHAT THEY LEARNED, LEARNING MORE, TEACHING, ETC. WE GREW A LOT OF OUR OWN MANAGEMENT TALENT THAT WAY.

(F) FOCUS ON HIRING RIGHT. WE HIRED VERY, VERY CAREFULLY, INTERVIEWING 12 TO 15 PEOPLE FOR EACH HIRE (EVEN WHEN WE HAD TO HIRE 30 PEOPLE AT A TIME). THAT'S BECAUSE WE WANTED TO TRUST THEM TO DO THEIR WORK INDEPENDENTLY WITHOUT MICROMANAGING THEM. WE HIRED PEOPLE WHO REALLY KNEW MORE THAN WE DID. WE USED TO SAY, "IF WE KNEW HOW TO DO YOUR JOB, WE'D DO IT. SO WE NEED YOU TO DEFINE IT FOR US AND WORK TO ACHIEVE WHAT WILL MAKE A DIFFERENCE FOR THE COMPANY. AND WE'LL TRUST YOU AS LONG AS YOU PRODUCE THOSE RESULTS." IT WAS ESSENTIAL THAT EVERY HIRE FIT WITH ALL OF THESE VALUES.

## CREATING THE SEVEN C'S OF CULTURE

*Culture* is the environment that influences how well people perform. Ideally, your culture will motivate and inspire outstanding performance from every individual in the company. Most entrepreneurs recognize the importance of culture, but it seems so abstract that they have a hard time understanding how to build it. Because many entrepreneurs think it's difficult to pinpoint the specific components and concrete actions that will actually create the culture they want, many of them fall into the trap of just letting culture develop on its own. When that happens, the culture can become scattered, negative, chaotic, and unhealthy. To avoid this pitfall, use your values as the foundation for culture building and be proactive about establishing processes that will consistently promote each of what we call the Seven C's of Culture (see box).

WHEN SOMEBODY ON YOUR TEAM DOES SOMETHING THAT EXEMPLIFIES GOOD ENTERPRISE LEADERSHIP, LET THEM KNOW THAT. DON'T MISS AN OPPORTUNITY TO TELL THEM. I THINK SOMETIMES AS COMPANY HEADS, WE WORRY A LOT ABOUT THE RANK AND FILE AND MAKING SURE THAT WE GIVE THEM FEEDBACK AND GIVE THEM RECOGNITION. AND WE MAY NOT WORRY AS MUCH ABOUT THE SENIOR EXECUTIVES, WHO PROBABLY NEED IT JUST AS MUCH, AND PARTICULARLY WHEN THEY'VE DEMONSTRATED REALLY GOOD LEADERSHIP. IT DOESN'T HAVE TO BE IN THEIR AREA. AND, IN FACT, IT PROBABLY ISN'T GOING TO BE IN THEIR FUNCTIONAL AREA. IT'S GOING TO BE CORPORATEWIDE. BUT GIVE THEM KUDOS AND LET THEM KNOW THEY'VE REALLY SET A GOOD EXAMPLE.

# VITAL SIGNS: THE SEVEN C'S OF CULTURE

**Customer and Market Focus:** Ensure that everyone constantly listens to, fully understands, and takes effective action to meet customers' and target markets' current and future needs.

**Communication:** Establish and consistently use open two-way channels—up, down, and across the organization—to make sure everyone knows what is expected of him or her, has enough information to make good decisions, communicates with other people involved with and affected by the decision, and has the opportunity to contribute feedback and ideas.

**Collaboration:** Develop and coordinate both functional and cross-functional teams that work effectively to accomplish mutual goals, solve problems, and move the company toward its vision.

**Creativity:** Continually tap people's brainpower with systematic methods for defining new opportunities and problems; challenge established practices; brainstorm options; manage and develop ideas; and generate fresh, innovative, and viable solutions.

**Continuous Learning:** Use knowledge, information, experiences, and feedback to build skills and increase the effectiveness of individual and corporate performance.

**Change Management:** Anticipate and use change for gain; encourage experimentation and create change.

**Constructive Leadership:** Require the CEO and all managers to align people and decisions with mission and goals, develop talent, build relationships, and motivate for maximum performance.

### Devising reward and recognition systems that reflect the core values

Sharing the financial rewards of the company with those who have lived by its values and produced the results is a powerful demonstration of how much you value your people, the key contributors to the company's success. Bonuses based on performance or results—including mechanisms such as profit sharing, stock options, phantom stock, or other forms of equity or equity-like compensation—give employees a meaningful sense of ownership and control. Also be creative in designing a variety of opportunities for nonmonetary recognition of individuals' and teams' contributions.

> Everybody wants wealth, and everybody wants to be rewarded. I was amazed at how morale shot up when we instituted a profit-sharing plan. All of a sudden, people were interested in the entire company, not just their individual jobs. They felt that their efforts were being rewarded directly, that, in a way, they were working for themselves. It supercharged the company and our growth.

# PERSONAL TRANSITIONS REQUIRED

Your new roles in the Continuous Growth stage mean not only growth for the company but growth for you as well. You will be stretching and changing along with your company. What follows are the six transitions you will need to make in your leadership style as your company moves through Continuous Growth.

## Make Strategy Your Major Focus

One transition will be to empower others to be accountable for all day-to-day operations while you focus largely on the strategic tasks of the company. These tasks require more external focus, so you will be spending more and more time away from the company. However, you will have to focus on the big-picture, critical internal issues as well, particularly on instilling the values, developing the organization, and building the innovative culture that make the company great. If you're going to build an extraordinary, legendary, and unique company that is admired for its growth and innovation, this is an incredibly important transition to make. At this stage and size of the company, you simply cannot lead the daily operations and still effectively guide the company to be future-focused and strategic.

I'M A BIG BELIEVER IN A "LEADERFUL" ORGANIZATION. THERE'S TOO MUCH GOING ON FOR ONE PERSON TO BE THE ONLY LEADER. THERE NEED TO BE A LOT OF LEADERS. ENTREPRENEURS ALWAYS SAY THEY WANT THAT, BUT THEY HAVE TO ENCOURAGE IT. I HAVE TO ENCOURAGE IT.

The challenges here are not dissimilar to those you experienced in moving from the Doer and Decision-Maker style of the Start-up stage to the Coach and Team-Builder roles in Rapid Growth:

# LET GO

The transition to let go isn't easy. It is difficult and frustrating to let go of what you're good at and/or what you're used to doing, especially if you see it as the fun stuff, *but you must let go.*

Resist the temptation to get sucked back into operations when people ask you for decisions about operational questions and want your direction on what they perceive as crises. Learn to turn those questions back to the people who will be accountable for them. Trust them to be competent and responsible in handling their tasks. That's the only way you can truly empower your managers and let everyone know who's really in charge of operational issues.

# WATCH YOUR TIMING

Choosing the correct time for stepping out of operations is the third transition. Your timing must be right. Don't take this step before your management team has all the right members or before it is operating constructively and creatively on its own. If you step away too soon, the company may stumble and stall without your day-to-day leadership, and you may have to step in again to focus on building and strengthening your team. Be careful not to fall into the classic pitfall of abdication versus delegation. No matter how tempting, do not give away or dump projects on others, with no follow-up. If you've built the right team, you should be able to delegate more and more of the day-to-day management of the company. But you always need to hold them accountable and responsible for the outcomes. From time to time, you'll need to check and make sure they are modeling the values and beliefs on which you're building the company. It's a delicate balance and requires good timing. Don't leave too soon. On the other hand, don't stay involved too long, or you may stifle the company and miss out on strategic opportunities because you're still deeply involved in day-to-day operations.

## MANAGE THE TRANSITION AND MANAGE THE CONTEXT

Managing the transition and its context can be frustrating and unsettling. At first it may feel like you have a lot of time on your hands. You may not be sure what to do with yourself. If you're like most entrepreneurs, you start missing that fun stuff, like designing new products or making sales calls to customers. But you need to focus on what it is that *only you* can do, and make the transition as quickly as possible to your new roles. Write down your new roles and goals. Think hard about what you need to do to take the company to the next level of growth. You'll get excited as you rediscover the external world and uncover the universe of new possibilities for the company in your role as Change Catalyst and Strategic Innovator. As Organization Builder and Chief of Culture, you'll have the opportunity to consider the best ways to create the right context for all employees by growing and strengthening the organizational design and cultural environment. These are tasks that only you can do, and they will become your new fun stuff.

IT'S DIFFICULT FOR PEOPLE TO CHANGE THROUGH ALL THE DIFFERENT STAGES OF THE COMPANY. IN THE BEGINNING, YOU DO ALL THE WORK YOURSELF. BUT THE NEXT STAGE IS TEACHING INSTEAD OF DOING. IT'S TRYING TO TEACH OTHERS HOW TO DO IT. THE STAGE BEYOND THAT IS PRESCRIBING RESULTS RATHER THAN TEACHING. IT'S SORT OF SAYING, "MAKE THIS HAPPEN. YOU KNOW HOW TO DO IT." THE FINAL LEVEL IS MANAGING THE CONTEXT. IN A LOT OF WAYS, MY JOB RIGHT NOW IS TO DEAL WITH THE VALUES AT THE COMPANY AND PUT IN SYSTEMS—LIKE COMPENSATION, RECRUITMENT, AND TRAINING— TO DEMONSTRATE THOSE VALUES. THERE'S BEEN A LOT TO LEARN AS A FOUNDER ABOUT REAL LEADERSHIP.

## SHARE LEADERSHIP WITH YOUR TEAM

You need to hold your entrepreneurial team accountable for sharing strategic leadership of the company with you. As you step out of operations, you must define the tasks of company leadership and make your executive team members responsible for thinking deeply and working with you on the company's strategic issues. Up to now, you have been the only person in the company with the big picture constantly on your mind. Your team has helped when called upon but has been primarily focused on their functional areas. Now you need them to help you create a new and better big-picture vision that includes their ideas as well. They'll bring in new perspectives and specialized knowledge you don't have; you'll see new sides of the picture you hadn't seen before. You and your team must share the challenge of developing and leading a new vision and strategy for growth, so the company can truly move on to an extraordinary level.

IN A RECENT OFF-SITE MEETING TO WORK ON A NEW VISION AND STRATEGY AFTER OUR IPO, I HAD TO FORCE MY EXECUTIVE TEAM MEMBERS TO PULL AWAY FROM THE SHORT-TERM, 18-MONTH PLANNING. WE SET UP THE MEETING SO THEIR DIRECT REPORTS FORMED TEAMS TO DEVELOP THOSE SHORT-TERM PLANS WHILE WE WENT OFF AS SENIOR MANAGEMENT TO EXPLORE OUR VIEW OF THE COMPANY IN THREE TO FIVE YEARS. IT WAS HARD FOR THEM TO GET THEIR HEADS AND HANDS OUT OF THE SHORTER-TERM PLANS, BUT WHEN WE HEARD WHAT THEIR MANAGERS CAME UP WITH, WE ALL REALIZED THAT THEY HAD CREATED AN OUTSTANDING PLAN THAT WOULD CAPITALIZE ON OUR STRENGTHS AND HELP US GROW FROM $30 MILLION TO $60 MILLION IN 18 MONTHS. THAT ALLOWED US TO FEEL FREED UP TO LOOK MUCH FURTHER OUT, AND TO SEE OUR COMPANY AS A $300 MILLION BUSINESS. THE EXECUTIVES HAVE SINCE BECOME CHAMPIONS OF THE LONG-TERM PLAN AND COACHES FOR THEIR MANAGERS TO CARRY OUT THE SHORT-TERM PLAN. THAT'S BEEN A BIG SWITCH FOR THEM.

TRAIN, TRAIN, TRAIN, AND THEN EMPOWER. NOT THE OTHER WAY AROUND. GIVE AUTONOMY WITH RESPONSIBILITY. ACCOUNTABILITY IS CRUCIAL. A MANAGE-MENT POSITION IS NOT A REWARD. IT'S A RESPONSIBILITY THAT REQUIRES UNIQUE SKILLS AND A WILLINGNESS TO PITCH IN ON THE BIG STRATEGIC MOVES AND DECISIONS.

It won't be easy. Here are some challenges that arise when you begin sharing leadership with your team.

## TEACHING YOUR TEAM TO PLAY MULTIPLE ROLES

When you first begin empowering your team in leadership roles, you may feel conflicted about asking them to take on so many roles at once. You want them to help define values to promote the culture, perform their functional jobs well, and assume the additional responsibility of working with you on new strategies for the company's future. They'll tell you they can't do it all. Your challenge is to listen to their concerns, but to be clear: You expect them to do it all, and they must learn to do it all. Tell them you expect them to set up their functional organizations in a way that permits handling both the operational and the strategic parts of their jobs. Instead of allowing the team members to be bottlenecks who impede growth, engage them in creative problem solving to alleviate their concerns while at the same time fulfilling the company's goals. Teach them to delegate appropriately and build bench strength in their staff.

WE HAVE COMPANYWIDE STAFF MEETINGS ABOUT EVERY MONTH OR SIX WEEKS. AND THERE'S SOME PREPARED MATERIAL FOR THAT, AND THEN THERE'S AN OPEN TOWN-MEETING KIND OF FORMAT; AND WE INVITE OUR "DOUBTING THOMASES" TO ASK THOSE TOUGH QUESTIONS THAT KIND OF MAKE ME BLANCH. BUT IT'S A GOOD THING FOR US. AND IN THOSE MEETINGS, I LIKE TO HAVE MEMBERS OF OUR EXECUTIVE TEAM TALK ABOUT A TOPIC THAT MAY OR MAY NOT BE WITHIN THEIR FUNCTIONAL AREA. IF IT IS, HAVE THEM EXPLAIN WHY IT'S SOMETHING THAT'S WORTHY OF A STAFF MEETING, BECAUSE IT IS OF ENTERPRISEWIDE IMPORTANCE, AND WHY IT IS THAT THEY'RE HANDLING IT THE WAY THEY ARE, AND GIVE THEM THE OPPORTUNITIES TO SHOW THAT LEADERSHIP.

AS MANY TIMES AS WE TALK ABOUT OBJECTIVES, AS MANY TIMES AS WE REVIEW THEM WITH THE STAFF, WITH ALL THE VOICE MAILS AND THE MEETINGS AND THE ONE-ON-ONES, IT'S NOT ENOUGH. YOU'VE GOT TO KEEP WORKING ON IT ALL THE TIME. AND THE CEO CAN'T DO IT ALONE. THE EXECUTIVE TEAM HAS TO HELP, HAS TO BE MESSENGERS OF THE VISION, INTERPRETERS OF THE VISION, AND WHAT I CALL OPEN-MINDED SUPPORTERS OF THE VISION. WHAT I MEAN IS THAT THEY CAN'T BE JUST MOUTHING THE PARTY LINE. THAT'S GOING TO HAVE ZERO CREDIBILITY WITH THE STAFF. THEY HAVE TO UNDERSTAND AND BUY INTO—AND LEAD—THE MISSION AND VISION FOR THE COMPANY.

## CONTINUALLY STRENGTHENING YOUR MANAGEMENT TEAM

Yet another challenge you will face during this period is the constant strengthening of your management team. As CEO you must be explicit about your expectations and creative about keeping the management team aligned. Nevertheless, you may still need to make the tough call that one or more team members are not suited for strategic leadership. During Continuous Growth, you must constantly evaluate your top team members, making sure you have a trusted team that can conduct operations while it shares strategic leadership with you. At the same time, you want to be sure your middle management is capable and empowered to help run the company operations. A great way to involve them and give responsibility is by chartering cross-functional teams to plan and problem-solve on critical company issues.

IT'S IMPORTANT TO DISCLOSE FINANCIAL RESULTS. WE DIDN'T ACTUALLY TALK ABOUT OUR FINANCIAL RESULTS UNTIL WE WERE AROUND 100 PEOPLE OR SO. WE WERE SECRETIVE ABOUT THAT STUFF. I REGRET THAT NOW. IT'S GOOD TO GET PEOPLE INVOLVED IN THE FINANCIAL RESULTS EARLY. YOU DON'T NECESSARILY HAVE TO SHOW THE BALANCE SHEET, BUT SHOWING THE INCOME STATEMENT IS PRETTY VALUABLE, AND HAVING SOMETHING RELEVANT LIKE A PROFIT-SHARING PROGRAM MAKES THEM INTERESTED IN THE COMPANY'S FINANCIAL RESULTS. AND THAT'S A REALLY IMPORTANT THING TO DO, BECAUSE THERE'S REAL VALUE IN GETTING PEOPLE TO UNDERSTAND THAT THEIR JOB IS TO MAKE THE BUSINESS MORE SUCCESSFUL AND THAT THEY GET DIRECT REWARDS FROM THAT. THEY NEED TO KNOW WHAT THE GAME IS.

## CONTINUALLY REINVENT AND REORGANIZE

The transition involved in reinventing and reorganizing is a difficult one. It involves challenging the company's current methods of achieving success and breaking the company's operating habits that worked so well in Rapid Growth. You must anticipate the company's needs for reinvention and the reorganization that accompanies it, recognize signals that it's time to move to a new level, and then push for change, possibly before others see the need. The pitfall is thinking that reorganization will be enough. However, reinvention means redefining the market focus, mission, vision, strategies, culture, and organizational structure. You can never be complacent.

During this period, you need to create a whole new vision and new ways of operating to reach that vision, trusting that those new methods are the right ones. Engage your entire team—with input from their staff and from outside the company—in discovering and developing a shared picture of new possibilities, identifying what needs to change and clearly articulating a plan for transformation and growth that everyone commits to implementing.

I HAD TO DO A LOT OF EVANGELIZING. BECAUSE THE COMPANY HAD BEEN SUCCESSFUL, GROWING FROM A LITTLE START-UP TO THE HIGH $20-MILLION RANGE, THERE WERE A LOT OF PEOPLE WHO THOUGHT WE SHOULDN'T BE CHANGING. THE BIGGEST HURDLE WAS GETTING THEM TO REALIZE THAT THE SUCCESS WE HAD AND THE IDEAS THAT LED TO IT WEREN'T VALID ANYMORE. SO I SPENT A LOT OF TIME, PERSONALLY, OUT WITH EMPLOYEES, REALLY GOING THROUGH THE THINKING, SHOWING FINANCIALS, SHOWING WHAT THE LIMITS WERE AND

WHY THE CURRENT BUSINESS WASN'T ANY GOOD. AND TRYING TO PAINT A BRIGHT PICTURE OF THIS NEW FUTURE. AND IT WAS QUITE CHOPPY. A LOT OF RESISTANCE. A LOT OF SKEPTICISM. WE LOST CUSTOMERS. AND WE LOST EMPLOYEES WHO HAD TO LEAVE THE COMPANY BECAUSE OF OUR OLD BUSINESS. THAT'S THE ONLY THING I REGRET. BUT WE KNEW WE'D HAVE TURMOIL AND TURNOVER. THAT'S PART OF THE PRICE WE KNEW WE WOULD HAVE TO PAY, PART OF THE INVESTMENT WE HAVE TO BE WILLING TO MAKE TO GROW THE COMPANY.

Continual reinvention brings clear challenges, and you need to be prepared for them.

## REALIZING THAT NEW GROWTH REQUIRES CHANGE

An IPO, an acquisition, or a major strategic partnership are all strategies for growth, but each can create huge, unanticipated problems.

It's difficult to know the ultimate impact of such events, but they often become major stumbling blocks because entrepreneurs frequently underestimate the fundamental need for a new plan. They tell their staff and customers that "Things won't really change all that much." But if you fail to realize how much change is needed, you will force your company into a reactive, crisis mode rather than proactive planning for reinvention. Think through the change very carefully, examine its implications, define a new picture of how the company will succeed, and put a specific action plan in place.

AFTER A YEAR'S WORTH OF EFFORT, WE DEVELOPED A SIGNIFICANT STRATEGIC PARTNERSHIP WITH IBM. IT WAS A WONDERFUL STRATEGIC DEAL, AND IT WAS EVERYTHING WE WANTED. BUT, FRANKLY, I DON'T THINK WE ANTICIPATED THE EXTENT TO WHICH WE NEEDED TO CHANGE. AND IT TOOK US MAYBE SIX MONTHS TO GO THROUGH THAT TRANSITION. WE HAD TO WORK THE RELATIONSHIP JUST TO FIND OUT WHAT DIDN'T WORK, AND THEN WE TRIED TO FIX IT. TODAY, I THINK IT WOULD TAKE US ABOUT SIX DAYS. I MEAN THAT LITERALLY. NOW I WOULD SAY TO MY TEAM: "HEY, WE'VE JUST PUT TOGETHER THIS STRATEGIC RELATIONSHIP. IT'S GOING TO CHANGE THINGS FOR US. LET'S IDENTIFY WHERE THOSE CHANGES ARE GOING TO COME FROM AND LET'S MANAGE IT. LET'S BE AHEAD OF IT."

## ACCEPTING THAT CHANGE IS CONSTANT

Growth may slow or stop if you don't have clarity about the vision and the right strategy for future growth. You may delay the company's reinvention by thinking that you must wait for a clear picture before starting the process. It's far better to push forward with your team and to work together to discover and crystallize the new vision and plan. Hanging on to the Rapid Growth success formula for too long is dangerous. The company cannot sustain the same path for too long and will succumb to external threats and/or internal dysfunction.

> I WENT THROUGH A VERY UNCOMFORTABLE TIME WHEN THE COMPANY HAD REACHED MY ORIGINAL VISION FOR IT AND I JUST COULDN'T PICTURE WHAT SHOULD HAPPEN NEXT. I SORT OF "FELL OFF" THE OTHER SIDE OF MY VISION, AND WE STARTED TO STAGNATE. INTERNALLY, WE GOT ON EACH OTHER'S NERVES AS WE REALIZED THE BUSINESS WAS SLOWING DOWN AND JUST DIDN'T EXCITE US AS MUCH ANYMORE.
>
> I FINALLY BROUGHT IN A CONSULTANT WHO HELPED THE TEAM TAKE A WHOLE NEW LOOK AT THE MARKET OPPORTUNITIES AND PRODUCT POSSIBILITIES. IT WAS THE TEAM THAT CREATED OUR NEW VISION FOR THE COMPANY'S GROWTH. WE CALL IT THE BIG IDEA, AND I'VE REGAINED MY EXCITEMENT ABOUT IT AS MY VISION. THERE ARE MANY CHANGES TO MAKE, BUT WE HAVE A SOLID PLAN FOR MAKING THEM HAPPEN AND WE'RE ON OUR WAY.

## LISTENING TO YOUR TEAM, EMPLOYEES, AND ADVISORS

Seeing a need for drastic change is not limited to the CEO. Many others in the company may see the need for revolutionary change before you do and wish you would take the plunge and make the change. In fact, they may wonder why it's taking you so long to "get it." You certainly don't want to become the emperor with no clothes! To avoid this pitfall, be the proactive driver who solicits feedback from both internal and external advisors and works with the executive team to create the kind of change that will carry the company to its full potential.

> ONE THING THAT IS ABSOLUTELY CRITICAL IS A THING I CALL RUF, RAW, UNVARNISHED FEEDBACK. YOU HAVE TO SOLICIT IT. YOU HAVE TO ACCEPT IT. AS A HUMAN, SOMETIMES YOU DON'T LIKE WHAT YOU HEAR. IT MIGHT MAKE YOU GRIND YOUR TEETH. IT MIGHT MAKE YOU WANT TO ROLL YOUR EYES. BUT YOU HAVE TO SOLICIT IT. YOU HAVE TO ACCEPT IT. YOU HAVE TO BE ABLE TO GIVE IT. A THING I DO TO HELP MY TEAM GIVE ME RUF (REMEMBER, TEAMS ARE UNNATURAL, PEOPLE AREN'T USED TO THIS) IS TO ASK THEM TO SOLICIT FEEDBACK FROM THEIR TEAMS. THEN THEY CAN COME BACK AND SAY, WELL, YOU KNOW MY TEAM THINKS THAT YOU WEREN'T CLEAR ON THUS AND SO. MAYBE THEY THINK THAT, TOO. BUT IT GIVES THEM A WAY, ALSO, TO START TO GIVE

THAT FEEDBACK. AND IF I ACCEPT IT IN AN OPEN-MINDED WAY, I THINK THAT HELPS REINFORCE THE FACT THAT WE ALL SHOULD BE DOING THAT WITH EACH OTHER.

YOU, AS CEO, OWN NOT ONLY THE VISION BUT THE EFFECTIVE EXECUTION OF THE GAME PLAN. THAT MEANS ALWAYS KEEPING YOUR EYE ON THE BALL, BUT— ESPECIALLY AS YOU GROW—IT ALSO MEANS KEEPING YOUR EYE ON THE FIELD. YOU HAVE TO BE ALERT SO THAT YOU SEE THE NEED FOR CHANGE WHEN IT ARISES, BUT YOU ALSO HAVE TO BE OPEN TO YOUR PEOPLE WHEN THEY SEE IT'S TIME TO MAKE RADICAL CHANGES. UNLESS YOU ARE, THEY'LL BE AFRAID TO BRING IT TO YOUR ATTENTION. THAT CAN MEAN DISASTER.

# APPLYING YOUR ENTREPRENEURIAL SKILLS

In Continuous Growth, your classic entrepreneurial strengths are every bit as important as they were when you first started your company. You have always been creative, visionary, and pioneering, constantly searching for new opportunities. As your company seeks new markets, new products, and new strategies, these qualities are vital to your ability to perform your roles as Change Catalyst and Strategic Innovator. Your strength in inspiring others continues to be critical as you move into your new roles as Chief of Culture and Organization Builder.

What's different is that you now have added the classic CEO skills of planning, communicating, team building, facilitating, and resolving conflict; and you are dedicated to constant learning. You can use this powerful combination of entrepreneurial strengths and CEO skills to lead the company through stage after stage of Continuous Growth. This is what constitutes your journey from entrepreneur to CEO.

SELF-ASSESSMENT IS ALWAYS IMPORTANT. AS YOU HIT ONE OF THESE PERIODS, STEP BACK, LOOK IN THE MIRROR AND SAY, "AM I PREPARED FOR THIS? BECAUSE I NEED TO TAKE A DEEP BREATH; I NEED ALL MY ENERGY. I'M GOING TO BE ABSOLUTELY IN THE LIMELIGHT. THE ORGANIZATION IS COUNTING ON ME NOW." AND I STRESS HERE THE VALUE OF MENTORS. MOST OF THE TIME, YOUR BOARD WILL NOT BE EFFECTIVE AS MENTORS. THEY HAVE A FIDUCIARY OBLIGATION, AND THERE ARE COMPLEXITIES IN RELATIONSHIPS WITH THE BOARD MEMBERS. YOU'LL BE BETTER OFF USING OTHER PEOPLE AS MENTORS.

YOUR VENTURE CAPITALISTS WILL SEE YOUR BUSINESS DIFFERENTLY THAN YOU DO. THEY WILL IMPOSE CHANGE ON YOUR ORGANIZATION. TRY TO FIND YOURSELF A MENTOR, OR MENTORS, WHO'VE BEEN DOWN THAT SAME PATH YOU'RE TAKING, WHO CAN GIVE YOU HONEST, OPEN FEEDBACK. IT'S INVALUABLE. I HAD THIS, AND IT WAS REALLY, REALLY HELPFUL TO ME.

IT'S HARD TO REMAIN A CEO IN A COMPANY. IT REALLY IS. YOU SEE SOME COMPANIES DOING GREAT, AND OTHERS CRASHING AND HAVING ALL SORTS OF TROUBLE. WHAT'S THE DIFFERENCE? LOOK TO SEE IF THE CEO IS LEARNING. THE ABILITY AND THE WILLINGNESS AND THE EAGERNESS TO LEARN IS THE SINGLE CORRELATING FACTOR WITH ONGOING SUCCESS AS A CEO.

IT'S ALWAYS IMPORTANT TO REMEMBER TO HAVE FUN. THAT'S THE PURPOSE OF ALL OF THIS, RIGHT? IT'S TO ENJOY OURSELVES, AND I'M HAVING A BLAST. LOOK AT YOUR COMPANY IN TERMS OF WHAT YOU THINK IS FUN AND WHAT YOUR PEOPLE THINK IS FUN. TRY TO KEEP THAT VIBRANCY ALIVE AND THAT PURSUIT OF DOING WHAT MAKES PEOPLE HAPPY.

I STARTED THE COMPANY BECAUSE I WANTED TO BUILD GREAT SOFTWARE PRODUCTS AND SHIP THEM AROUND THE WORLD AND HAVE ENOUGH MONEY COME IN SO I COULD WIND SURF AND CONTINUE TO WRITE SOFTWARE. AFTER ABOUT FIVE YEARS, THOUGH, I LEARNED TO HAVE A NEW INTEREST: BUILDING ORGANIZATIONS AND THE TEAMS TO RUN THEM. I HAD NO INTEREST IN THAT IN THE EARLY DAYS. IT WAS A NUISANCE. I WAS NOT PROACTIVE ABOUT GROWTH, AND I WAS SORT OF DRAGGED THROUGH A SERIES OF ACTIVITIES TO MOVE FORWARD. THEN I DISCOVERED SOMETHING IMPORTANT. AN ORGANIZATION IS LIKE SOFTWARE. IT CAN BE DESIGNED. IT'S A DYNAMIC SYSTEM. IT BECAME MY SECOND PASSION IN LIFE: TO BUILD A GREAT PLACE TO WORK, TO BUILD GREAT TEAMS, AND TO FOCUS ON THE ORGANIZATIONAL DETAILS AS AN END UNTO THEMSELVES. THAT CERTAINLY WASN'T TRUE WHEN I FIRST STARTED.

I'M PART OF WHAT'S CALLED A FORUM, A GROUP OF A DOZEN OR SO CEOS WHO SHARE EVERYTHING GOING ON IN THEIR BUSINESS AND PERSONAL LIVES WITH ONE ANOTHER, IN A VERY CONFIDENTIAL SETTING. IT'S A VALUABLE RESOURCE, AND IF YOU DON'T HAVE ONE OF THESE, I WOULD JUST SAY SEEK

ONE OUT. PUT IT ON YOUR ACTION LIST. IT CAN MAKE SUCH A BIG DIFFERENCE. YOU HAVE TO RECOGNIZE, NUMBER ONE, THAT YOU MUST BE OPEN TO YOUR PEERS' FEEDBACK AND RECOGNIZE THAT SHARING YOUR ISSUES WILL LEAD MANY TIMES TO A CLEARER PERSPECTIVE ON YOUR PART, AND BETTER DECISION MAKING. I'M ABSOLUTELY CONVINCED OF THAT. DURING THESE PERIODS OF RAPID CHANGE, YOU HAVE THE LEAST AMOUNT OF SUPPORT FROM YOUR NORMAL INTERNAL NETWORKS, SO IT'S GOOD TO FIND A NETWORK ON THE OUTSIDE THAT CAN PROVIDE THAT SUPPORT.

PEOPLE TEND TO FOLLOW ME BECAUSE THEY THINK I'M SMART, I KNOW WHERE I'M GOING, AND I MUST HAVE A REASON AND A PLAN FOR GETTING THERE. THAT'S INCREDIBLY VALUABLE WHEN IT COMES TO RUNNING MY BUSINESS, BUT IT MEANS I CONSTANTLY HAVE TO LEARN NEW SKILLS AND BUILD FRESH PERSONAL PERSPECTIVES. OTHERWISE, MY MESSAGES GET OLD, PEOPLE WILL THINK I'VE LOST TOUCH, AND IT WILL BECOME MUCH HARDER FOR ME TO GET THEM TO FOLLOW MY LEADERSHIP.

THERE ARE SO MANY WAYS TO SCREW UP A YOUNG COMPANY, AND MOST ARE RELATED TO PEOPLE AND MANAGEMENT. WE ENTREPRENEURS THINK THAT ENTREPRENEURSHIP IS ABOUT BUILDING A PRODUCT AND PIONEERING A MARKET, AND WHAT WE HAVE TO LEARN IS THAT IT IS ALSO ABOUT BUILDING AN ORGANIZATION. IT'S ABOUT MANAGEMENT AND PEOPLE AND LEVERAGING THE STRENGTHS AND EXPERIENCE OF NONENTREPRENEURS.

# SUMMARY:
# CONTINUOUS GROWTH STAGE

## COMPANY GOALS

- Dominate the industry.

- Jump to the next curve.

- Move to a whole new level of success by changing the growth strategy and reinventing how the company operates.

- Expand to new markets and grow new niches in current markets.

- Add products and services to provide more "total solutions" for customers.

- Brand the company and its people as thought leaders.

## COMPANY CHARACTERISTICS

- Organization has grown significantly and has the potential to be an industry leader.

- Competitive threats, customer demands, and technology changes pose ever more complicated challenges.

- The company has outgrown its plan and infrastructure.

- The company is executing, or considering, new growth strategies: acquisitions, strategic alliances, IPOs, spinoffs, new product lines, etc.

*cont...*

-CONTINUED

## RED FLAGS: SIGNALS FOR CHANGING YOUR ROLE

- As you spend more and more time outside the company, you worry about your management team's ability to run the business without you.

- You need to solve much more complex problems, and the old ways of handling them don't work.

- The organization seems unwieldy and is entering turbulence.

- You don't have enough time for vital strategic tasks; you wonder whether you need a COO to run operations.

- People don't seem to understand the new growth strategy or share your sense of urgency about the demands for fundamental change.

- You believe in the need for change but also worry about throwing the company into chaos with too much change.

- It feels like you're constantly communicating, but managers complain that they don't understand decisions or how they were made.

- People accuse you of micromanaging and not empowering them.

- Keeping an entrepreneurial culture seems impossible.

- People you count on and want to keep are leaving the company.

### DANGERS IF YOU DON'T CHANGE

- Company will start to spin its wheels, lose focus on the big picture, and hit a wall.

- You won't know what hit you.

- New competition will erode your market share; revenue and profits will fall.

- People will return to a reactive crisis mode.

- Company will spin out of control and become another crash-and-burn victim.

### KEY LEADERSHIP ROLES

- Change Catalyst

- Organization Builder

- Strategic Innovator

- Chief of Culture

### CRITICAL RESPONSIBILITIES

- Recognize the need for fundamental change and proactively lead the discovery and implementation of a strategic plan for achieving dramatic new growth.

- Develop the executive team so that each member becomes a company leader; empower the team to run day-to-day operations while you focus only on strategic issues.

*cont...*

-CONTINUED

- Establish a network of teams for bottom-up planning and operations.

- Provide the company with an objective, expanded view of the external environment.

- Find and develop high-level partnerships and relationships to leverage for growth.

- Use a written set of core values to guide everyone's behavior; devise reward and recognition programs to reinforce these values.

- Establish systematic processes to consistently promote the "7 C's of Culture."

## PERSONAL CHANGES TO MAKE IN YOUR LEADERSHIP ROLE

- Spend all your time working on the big picture, not on the day-to-day aspects of the business.

- Step out of operations and make strategy and culture your main focus.

- Hold your team accountable for sharing strategic leadership with you.

- Push for the continual reinvention and the periodic planning and reorganization required for new growth.

- Redefine and constantly develop the culture that will attract and retain the best performers.

# CHAPTER 5

# KEEPING IT ALL IN PERSPECTIVE

**At this point, you may be feeling overwhelmed. Perhaps you are asking yourself whether you can handle all the changes needed to successfully lead your company through these stages of growth. You may be wondering whether you have what it takes to make the transformation from founding entrepreneur to entrepreneurial CEO.**

## KNOWLEDGE IS SUCCESS

Successful entrepreneurial leaders say that in order to manage each stage of your company's growth, you need to know eight things: yourself, your role, your company, your customers, your environment, your people, your future, and your potential.

## WHAT YOU HAVE TO KNOW

**Know Yourself**

- Clarify your personal values and goals, and understand the psyche of an entrepreneur. Learn to manage your ups and downs, your time and your health.

- Manage your relationships with family, friends, and community.

- Be conscious and observant of your effectiveness in your role as a leader.
- Assess your strengths and weaknesses, set your goals, and develop a game plan to learn what you need to know to be a successful and effective entrepreneurial CEO.

## Know Your Role

- Commit to the multiple responsibilities and requirements in each stage of growth.
- Recognize and balance the expectations from all constituencies.
- Acknowledge the enormous power of the CEO role, and use it wisely to influence the behavior you want.

## Know Your Company

- Know your markets, the value of your products/services, and why customers buy.
- Identify the stage you're in: Start-up, Initial Growth, Rapid Growth, or Continuous Growth and take on the roles and responsibilities for that stage.
- Establish the vision and growth strategy necessary to manage the current stage and move to the next stage.

## Know Your Customers

- Build close relationships, which will lead to opportunities for innovation.
- Learn their problems and goals for the future, and use them as a guide to your new product development.
- Help them gain their competitive advantage as your competitive advantage.

## Know Your Environment

- Watch trends and recognize their impact as threats or opportunities.
- Build systems to continuously scan for information and changes.
- Use this information in your planning process.

## Know Your People

- Carefully select the people you want.
- Get to know them and be accessible.

- Develop methods to continuously communicate with them.

- Assess their performance, provide feedback, and develop them as leaders of growth.

**Know Your Future**

- Anticipate and plan for the three stages of growth.

- Create the vision and then update it each year.

- Prepare for the changes you will need to make when redefining your role as leader.

**Know Your Potential**

- Understand your unique abilities and your areas needing development.

- Get feedback regularly; don't be blind to how you're perceived.

- Learn continually.

- Create action plans for your own development and hold yourself accountable.

# KEYS TO LEADING AT THE SPEED OF GROWTH

Many of the entrepreneurial skills and attitudes that have brought you this far can carry you further than you'd ever have dreamed. The self-confidence that allows you to take risks shunned by others, your constant focus on the future, your passion, your energy, and your ability to solve problems and have fun will stand you in good stead as you make the necessary changes in your leadership style. Through this book, you've learned from other entrepreneurs who have managed high growth. You now have the keys to high-growth leadership, or what we call *leading at the speed of growth*. Use the following 10 keys as you progress from founding entrepreneur to successful entrepreneurial leader of a high-growth company.

## 1. BE AN ORGANIZATION BUILDER

Great entrepreneurial leaders see their job as creating an organization in which extremely talented people want to work and where quality customers want to do business. This job is very different from making and selling the product or service upon which the company was founded. It requires you, the leader, to accomplish the following:

- Determine and communicate your own values and philosophies; decide what culture you want to create.

- Create clarity in the organization: clarity of purpose, direction, structure, measurement and consequences.

- Help others be successful.

- Monitor the hiring process. Make sure you hire people with your values, people who are self-motivated and can describe how working in your company will help them reach their own goals.

- Provide appropriate reward systems.

- Create an experimental learning attitude.

- Celebrate victories.

## 2. ANTICIPATE TRANSITIONS AND GUIDE THE COMPANY THROUGH THEM

Think ahead and help the entire company anticipate the transitions required for moving to new stages of growth. Make these transitions, and make the necessary changes in your own role and style, as soon as possible. Always keep the vision in front of everyone; update it regularly with your team to make sure it is a shared dream that is exciting and compelling for all of you. Create a plan that includes market focus, mission, values, vision, strategies, structure, and culture. Being proactive is essential to getting the right financing, people, systems, new products, acquisitions, and reinvention plans in place so you don't hit the wall.

## 3. HIRE AND LEVERAGE AWESOME PEOPLE

Hire smart, self-motivated people you respect and trust. Share your vision, goals, and values with them. Delegate responsibilities to them, and encourage them to be proactive in helping the company grow. It's not as hard to let go if you have trusted people ready to take on new responsibilities. Select people for their cultural fit first and then their skills. Build in accountability for the right tasks and values required in the job. Learn how to pull ideas from all parts of the organization so you can fully capitalize on everyone's talents. Use your management team to expand your leadership capacity and make sure the members are developing leaders in their own departments. Do what it takes to keep your awesome people committed to staying with you to grow the company.

## 4. USE YOUR ENTREPRENEURIAL STRENGTHS TO BUILD LEADERSHIP SKILLS

Recognize that your own characteristics as an entrepreneur can be both strengths and weaknesses. Be fully aware of their impact and apply them in appropriate ways as your leadership role changes.

No matter what stage your company is in, the classic entrepreneurial strengths you can count on are the ability to see new possibilities, take on new challenges, and find creative solutions to meet those challenges. These strengths will help you make the necessary personal transitions as you see new opportunities for growth, create new visions for the company and yourself, and proactively develop the new skills required for your job.

Once you've gained the capabilities for planning, communicating, listening, coaching, team building, resolving conflicts, integrating the ideas of others, and building the organization, you can transform from the "typical" entrepreneur to a great entrepreneurial CEO. In this capacity, you can create the innovative culture that stimulates everyone to use their own entrepreneurial strengths as they seek new challenges and creatively solve them.

## 5. STICK TO YOUR VALUES

Articulating the values you believe in is vital to achieving successful growth. Know what you will and won't tolerate, and never, never compromise. If you ignore the values, you send a clear message to everyone that these values are not really important after all.

## 6. LOOK IN THE MIRROR

Look in the mirror and know your strengths and weaknesses. Part of becoming a great entrepreneurial leader is engaging in serious and frequent self-assessment to evaluate how you're doing. Identify the gaps in accomplishment of your goals and the effectiveness of your decisions, as well as the appropriateness of your style and behaviors that reinforce your values. Then determine what should change and take action to fill those gaps. Find ways to analyze your effectiveness and avoid at all costs the trap of blindness!

## 7. Get Feedback from Your Top Team and Employees

One of the most important characteristics of any great leader—and unfortunately, one of the rarest—is the ability to solicit and absorb candid feedback from his or her team. Feedback is easy to get from outsiders, such as customers or board members, but honest feedback is much more difficult to get from employees and even your own managers. So you must push your people to give you the feedback you need to gauge your own effectiveness as a leader, as well as your decisions and ideas for the company. Don't fall into the trap of allowing people to tell you what you want to hear, or you will be perceived as a boss right out of Dilbert: a poor leader.

## 8. Use Mentors, Coaches, and Peers for Counsel and Advice

You have already learned how lonely the job of leader can be. So it's critical to find mentors, advisors, and peers who can offer ideas and act as a sounding board on those issues you don't want to discuss with people inside the company. Many entrepreneurs find it useful to have a board of advisors—almost an informal board of directors—upon whom they can regularly call for counsel and advice. You can also hire outside professionals to bring skills to your company that are not found internally. Their expertise is worth their fees because they have often been through similar situations that you are encountering for the first time.

## 9. Be a Continual Learner

As one entrepreneur told us, "The ability, willingness, and eagerness to learn is the single correlating factor with ongoing success as a CEO; those who keep learning can grow and can lead a growing company." Put yourself in perpetual "discovery" mode and seek every opportunity to learn about yourself, other people, the business you're in, new skills, new products, market dynamics, trends, and other vital information. Make sure you learn all the things you need to learn. Everything you learn can be used to build your own strengths as a leader as well as your company's. You also need to model this "continual learner" behavior for people in your organization. How can you expect the company to grow if your people aren't learning new things? And how can you expect people to learn if you're not learning yourself?

This kind of continuous learning and self-development does not mean simply "being open" to ideas other people propose. Instead, it requires you to be proactive about trying to push the envelope, see outside the box, set goals for yourself, and then find the best ways to add to the competencies of the company and you, its leader.

When learning a new competency, it's useful to remember that education experts have identified four distinct stages of learning. In *unconscious incompetence,* you don't know what you don't know. You can't do the job, don't even know what the job requires; in short, you're clueless. On the other hand, *conscious incompetence* means that even though you may not be able to do the job, at least you recognize that you aren't performing as expected. You're aware that you need to learn more. As you learn, practice, evaluate, make progress, improve, and build new skills, you enter *conscious competence.* You are conscious of what makes you competent and you work at getting better and better in your role. In the last stage, *unconscious competence,* you have internalized the new skills and behavior, the values and beliefs, to the point that they come naturally without your even thinking about them. You may not be conscious of your decisions, but you operate at a high level of competence—and you are a role model for others.

## 10. HAVE FUN AND ENJOY THE RIDE

Remember all your reasons for starting the company in the first place: to have more independence and autonomy, to create something big that had never been done before, and to have fun. Don't ever lose your sense of humor and your zest for leading your high-growth company. It will provide a never-ending set of challenges and plenty of opportunities to laugh, cry, and grow. Learn how to ride the tiger, rather than be eaten alive by it.

# ENTREPRENEUR'S GUIDE TO COMMON PITFALLS

We've discussed some of the problems and dilemmas that can arise as you move your company from Start-up to Initial Growth, through Rapid Growth, and, eventually, to Continuous Growth. Here are the pitfalls and mistakes our entrepreneurs identified as the most common roadblocks they encountered in building their companies.

## NOT KNOWING WHAT TO EXPECT

Never having grown a company before, many entrepreneurs are unaware of the need for change. Many of those we interviewed admitted to being clueless when they began and wished they had made fundamental changes, such as hiring, financing, and building infrastructure, much sooner. After hitting a wall and finding out all they could do was react, they learned that some crises are not necessary and can be avoided by being proactive (see the following figure).

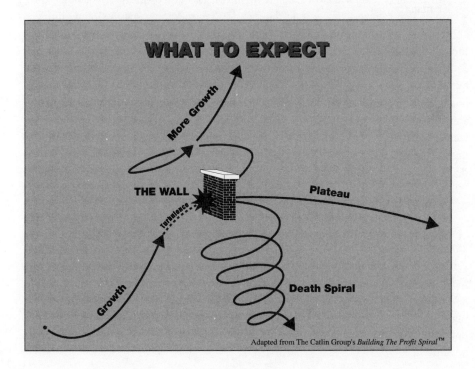

**WHAT TO EXPECT**

More Growth

THE WALL

Plateau

Turbulence

Growth

Death Spiral

Adapted from The Catlin Group's *Building The Profit Spiral*™

## THINKING THAT DIFFICULT ISSUES ARE "PART OF NORMAL GROWING PAINS" AND THUS UNAVOIDABLE

Some problems are "normal," and we've tried to identify them in this book. But many aren't normal. Don't assume that a certain amount of chaos and trauma are required in order to grow a company. Chaos and trauma are very tough and expensive ways to learn! You do not have to "live with" problems such as personality differences, values conflicts, team dysfunctions, or attitude problems. It's important to be creative in finding solutions to these seemingly impossible problems.

# THINKING THAT PAST BEHAVIOR WILL ENSURE FUTURE SUCCESS

The typical entrepreneur is perceived as relying on seat-of-the-pants management, "winging-it," having multiple priorities, and always doing new things. This kind of leader manages for the present, not the future; changes direction at the drop of a hat; chases any and all opportunities; and doesn't trust others to make decisions. These traits and habits can help you succeed in the early stages of Initial Growth, but you must break them as the company grows—or you will inhibit your company's growth. The habits that have led to your initial success are especially difficult to break. It's hard to fathom that the very behavior that contributed to your success at one stage can cause you to stall out or fail at the next. But it can, and it will.

# BEING UNAWARE OF HOW OTHERS PERCEIVE YOU

Being blind to how others see you can be a leader's fatal flaw. The people around you, both inside and outside the company, can see your strengths and weaknesses and have ideas about how you need to change to become more effective. Your classic entrepreneurial strengths may become your biggest weaknesses if people think your actions are off-base or are destructive to the company's potential success. It's a terrible irony that some entrepreneurs become the kind of tyrannical autocrats they dislike and are completely unaware of how they appear to others. Blind leaders demotivate people, stifle innovation, and dramatically limit a company's growth potential.

# NOT LISTENING

Many entrepreneurs have a hard time listening to the ideas of others. You need to balance your self-confidence with a willingness to listen to, and incorporate, other people's perspectives, feedback, ideas, and visions. Unless you learn to integrate ideas and perspectives from others into your decisions, plans, and actions, the company will not be able to grow beyond the scope of your capacity. You will become the bottleneck, rather than the leader, of company growth.

# FAILING TO FOCUS THE COMPANY

Lack of clarity about the company's direction, priorities, targeted opportunities, expectations, and values leads to confusion and lots of wheel spinning without solid results. People need to be focused and engaged in activities that meet the needs of key customers and target markets. When entrepreneurs won't follow their plan, make the hard choices about strategy, and are overly responsive to customers, suppliers, analysts, or stockholders, employees become confused and distracted. The result is that the company begins to stall and even spiral downward.

## NOT COMMUNICATING ENOUGH

Many entrepreneurs are not good communicators. They keep people in the dark about their vision, plans, and decisions. Often, they think they have communicated enough, when in fact they haven't even scratched the surface. This pitfall arises from failing to make vision and alignment the number-one priority of leadership.

## MISMANAGING NEW HIRES

Many entrepreneurs hire people for their skills but then mismanage and stifle their potential. You need to delegate appropriately, but giving new hires free rein too early is another pitfall. Before you let new hires operate independently, be sure they learn and practice the values that are important to you and that they operate in sync with the company's culture. If they follow the culture of their past companies instead of yours, their decisions and activities may not fit with the company you're growing. This is likely to happen when many people are hired quickly to fill slots.

To avoid such a pitfall, make sure you hire people based on their values first, skills second. Then participate in the orientation of new hires and make sure they are integrated into the culture. Teach them "the way we do things around here." Discuss your expectations for their performance, coach them on how to operate as a member of the team, listen to their observations and ideas, and then hold them accountable for results, team interactions, and the behaviors you want. Once they're fully integrated and you trust them to make decisions and take action appropriately, delegate to them and eventually give them the freedom and the responsibility to be entrepreneurial and independent.

## AVOIDING TOUGH DECISIONS

Leaders have many difficult responsibilities. Even when they know what the decision has to be, many entrepreneurs procrastinate, especially when the issue involves giving negative feedback to people who are not performing. When people can't perform their jobs or don't fit their roles, they must be reassigned to another job or moved out of the company. Other tough issues occur when strategic changes must be made to enable the company to move to a new level, but the risks of those decisions are perceived as too high. Trying to hold on and continue the current path to avoid these risks can seriously delay the company's growth. Instead, engage your team in planning for reinvention and renewal.

## FAILING TO ADD NEW SKILLS AND KNOWLEDGE TO YOUR ENTREPRENEURIAL REPERTOIRE

The success of the company is all about leadership and learning to fully maximize your leadership capacity. If you're not learning, you can't change and the company cannot grow. It takes hard work and requires considerable self-awareness to become the leader your company needs at each stage of its development. You must constantly assess where you are, anticipate the need for change, and proactively guide your company to ever-higher levels. No matter which stage you're in, there will be areas where you are less competent than others, and you'll just have to work on changing your behavior and developing new skills and knowledge.

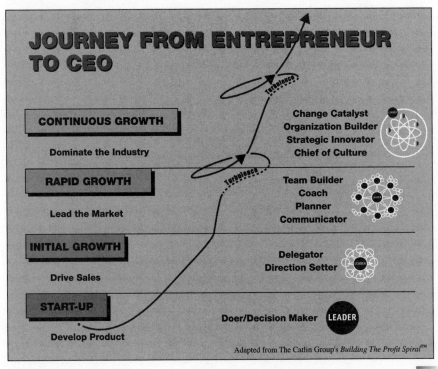

## JOURNEY FROM ENTREPRENEUR TO CEO

**CONTINUOUS GROWTH**
Dominate the Industry

**RAPID GROWTH**
Lead the Market

**INITIAL GROWTH**
Drive Sales

**START-UP**
Develop Product

Change Catalyst
Organization Builder
Strategic Innovator
Chief of Culture

Team Builder
Coach
Planner
Communicator

Delegator
Direction Setter

Doer/Decision Maker  **LEADER**

Adapted from The Catlin Group's *Building The Profit Spiral*™

Nobody said it would be easy to take on new roles, identify developmental needs, set goals, absorb new ideas and best practices, experiment, evaluate, modify, practice, and seek feedback. You need a variety of sources to learn from, including peers, conferences, books, mentors, advisors, and your own managers, employees, and customers.

But you can do it, if you capitalize on your entrepreneurial strengths, set new challenges, create new possibilities, and use your curiosity, innovation, and creativity. Take the time to learn from your experiences and defining moments, as well as the experiences of other entrepreneurs. You will stumble at times, just as the entrepreneurs who shared their stories with us often did. But as you make the journey from entrepreneur to CEO (see the preceding figure), regard each stumble as part of the continuous learning process that will help you develop into the leader your company needs now—and the great leader it will need in the future.

# INDEX